GREAT TASTES

BBQ

First published in 2010 by Bay Books, an imprint of Murdoch Books Pty Limited

Murdoch Books Australia
Pier 8/9
23 Hickson Road
Millers Point NSW 2000
Phone: +61 (0) 2 8220 2000
Fax: +61 (0) 2 8220 2558
www.murdochbooks.com.au

Murdoch Books UK Limited
Erico House, 6th Floor
93–99 Upper Richmond Road
Putney, London SW15 2TG
Phone: +44 (0) 20 8785 5995
Fax: +44 (0) 20 8785 5985
www.murdochbooks.co.uk

Chief Executive: Juliet Rogers
Publishing Director: Kay Scarlett
Publisher: Lynn Lewis
Senior Designer: Heather Menzies
Designer: Clare O'Loughlin
Production: Kita George
Index: Jo Rudd

ISBN: 9781741968743

PRINTED IN CHINA

OVEN GUIDE: You may find cooking times vary depending on the oven you are using. For fan-forced ovens, as a general rule, set the oven temperature to 20°C (35°F) lower than indicated in the recipe.

GREAT TASTES

BBQ

More than 120 easy recipes for every day

bay books

CONTENTS

BBQ BASICS

Types of barbecue

There are two main methods of cooking on a barbecue. The first is to cook food over direct heat, such as over a wood fire or barbecue fuel briquettes located directly under a grill or plate. The food must be turned during cooking so that it cooks evenly on both sides.

The other method is to use indirect heat, for which you need a barbecue with some kind of hood or cover. This method of cooking works a bit like an oven, by circulating the heat around the food, and it is mainly used for roasting larger cuts of meat, giving them a distinctive barbecue flavour.

Wood-burning fixed barbecues are the traditional, backyard barbecue — usually a fairly simple construction in the form of an elevated grill plate with a fire burning underneath. Although easy to use and available to anyone with clear space, a few bricks and a grill, the basic design lends itself only to fairly simple methods of cooking. Heat regulation is usually achieved by adjusting the fire and waiting for it to reach the right temperature, although it's preferable to let the flames die down and cook over a pile of glowing embers which give off a more constant heat.

Kettle barbecues are portable, come in a range of sizes and are designed for both direct and indirect cooking. A kettle barbecue has a rounded base which holds barbecue fuel briquettes on a metal grill. If you want to cook with direct heat, simply grill the food over the coals. If you want to cook using the indirect method, arrange the briquettes in two piles on opposite sides of the bottom grill and put a drip-tray between them before inserting the top grill. To give the heat a boost, open the vents in the outer shell of the barbecue — this will allow air to circulate, making the briquettes burn faster and hotter. To keep the temperature a little cooler, you must leave the vents closed.

Gas barbecues are available in a huge variety of sizes and shapes, from small portables to huge, wagon-style barbecues that come with a hood, rotisserie and workbench on the side. They are convenient and simple to operate, usually requiring only 10 minutes or so to heat up, and the turn of a knob to regulate temperature. Some work by means of a flame under the barbecue plate, while others use the flame to heat a bed of reusable volcanic rock. If your barbecue has a lid or hood, you can also cook using indirect heat.

Electric barbecues operate on a principle similar to that of gas barbecues, by heating the grill plate on which the food is cooked. They can be less convenient than a gas barbecue as they require access to an electricity outlet and the heat they produce may not be as even or as strong as that produced by a gas or solid-fuel barbecue.

Methods of cooking

Indirect and direct are the main cooking methods when you are using a barbecue. Make sure you set up your barbecue properly to shorten cooking times and make sure that all your lovingly prepared meals are perfectly cooked.

For direct cooking

KETTLE BARBECUE: Start the barbecue and let the briquettes burn for about 45 minutes before you begin cooking. For a medium–hot barbecue, use about 60, for a lower temperature, about 45 briquettes should be enough. If you need to lower the temperature when the fire is already set, just spritz the coals with a light spray of water, but if you want to increase the heat, you will need to add more briquettes and wait for the heat to develop.

GAS OR ELECTRIC BARBECUE: Light the barbecue and leave it to heat for about 10 minutes before cooking.

For indirect cooking

KETTLE BARBECUE: Start the barbecue (putting the fuel on each side to leave room for the drip tray) and leave the fire to develop for about 45 minutes. Put a drip tray between the coals and sit the top grill in place. Position the food so that it is over the drip tray and cover it with the lid. Keep the bottom vents open so that the heat circulates evenly, and don't open the lid unless it's really necessary — the more often the heat is allowed to escape, the longer your cooking time will be.

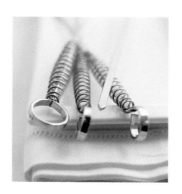

GAS OR ELECTRIC BARBECUE: It is always best to check the manufacturers' instructions on how to set up your barbecue for indirect cooking. In general, the outside burners are set to medium—low and the food sits in the middle of the barbecue. This means that the heat can circulate around the meat without burning it underneath.

BBQ tips

- Food cooked on a grill plate can also be cooked on an open grill provided it is large enough not to fall through the holes.

- Food cooked on an open grill may also be cooked on a grill plate.

- Invest in a small fire extinguisher, in case of emergency.

- For best results, bring the meat to room temperature before cooking it, but it is not advisable to leave it sitting at room temperature for more than 20 minutes.

- Always make sure that your barbecue is clean before lighting it. If possible, clean it out as soon as it is cool enough to do so, brushing or scraping the grill plates and discarding ash and embers.

- Assemble all the equipment you will need before you start cooking so that you won't have to leave the food unattended.

- Make sure that the barbecue is in a sheltered position and on a level surface, away from wooden fences, overhanging trees or anything else that may be flammable.

- Brush or spray the barbecue with oil before lighting it in case the oil comes in contact with the flame and flares up. To stop food from sticking, brush it with oil just before cooking it, make sure the grill plate is the correct temperature and don't turn the food until the surface of the food has cooked and 'released' itself naturally from the grill.

- If you wish to use the marinade to baste, you must boil it, then let it simmer for at least 5 minutes before basting so that any bacteria from the raw meat are not transferred to the cooked meat.

- If you are basting the food with a sugary glaze, apply it only in the last 10 minutes of cooking, as it will tend to burn on the grill.

- Always soak wooden skewers for at least 30 minutes before use to prevent them from charring on the grill.

- Salt meat just before barbecuing as salt will quickly draw moisture out of the meat if it is left.

Cooking time guide

The cooking temperature in a kettle or covered barbecue is not always constant, so we've provided these times to use as a guide (500 g = 1 lb 2 oz).

Beef per 500 g	with a bone	boneless
rare	15 minutes	10 minutes
medium	20 minutes	15 minutes
well–done	25 minutes	20 minutes

Leg of lamb per 500 g	
medium–rare	10–15 minutes
medium	20–25 minutes
well done	30 minutes

Pork

Allow 30 minutes per 500 g

Pork should be cooked through, but not overcooked or the flesh will be dry. Test that it is ready by inserting a skewer into the thickest part of the pork, or close to the bone; the juices should be clear with no trace of pink.

Poultry

Allow 20–25 minutes per 500 g

It's important that chicken is cooked right through with no pink flesh or juices inside. Check by inserting a skewer between the thigh and the body through to the bone; the juices should run clear.

Fish

Allow 20–25 minutes per 500 g

Different varieties of fish require different cooking times. Tuna and salmon steaks are often cooked medium–rare, as the flesh can become dry if cooked through. Depending on thickness, they may only need a few minutes on each side over direct heat. Most other fish are served cooked through. It is important to remove them from the barbecue as soon as they are ready, as residual heat in the flesh will continue to cook the meat. Test by inserting a thin-bladed knife into the thickest part of the fish; it will be ready when the flesh flakes cleanly.

SKEWERS & SAUSAGES

MEDITERRANEAN CHICKEN SKEWERS

MAKES 8 SKEWERS

2 large chicken breast fillets, cut into 32 cubes

24 cherry tomatoes

6 cap mushrooms, cut into quarters

2 garlic cloves, crushed

zest of 1 lemon, grated

2 tablespoons lemon juice

2 tablespoons olive oil

1 tablespoon oregano leaves, chopped

1   Soak eight wooden skewers in water to prevent scorching. Thread a piece of chicken onto each skewer, followed by a tomato, then a piece of mushroom. Repeat twice for each skewer and finish with a piece of chicken. Put the skewers in a shallow, non-metallic dish.

2   Combine the garlic, lemon zest, lemon juice, olive oil and chopped oregano, pour over the skewers and toss well. Marinate for at least 2 hours, or overnight if time permits.

3   Cook the skewers on a hot, lightly oiled barbecue grill or flatplate for 4 minutes on each side, basting occasionally, until the chicken is cooked.

LAMB SKEWERS WITH YOGHURT SAUCE

SERVES 4

8 lamb fillets, trimmed and cut into
  2.5 cm (1 inch) cubes

2 tablespoons olive oil

80 ml (2½ fl oz/⅓ cup) lemon juice

2 garlic cloves, crushed

2 teaspoons dried mint leaves

YOGHURT SAUCE

250 g (9 oz/1 cup) thick Greek-style
  yoghurt

1 garlic clove, crushed

1 **Put the lamb** in a non-metallic bowl with the olive oil, lemon juice, garlic and mint. Stir the pieces around until well coated and season with black pepper. Cover and refrigerate for at least 4 hours, or overnight.

2 **Make the yoghurt sauce** by mixing the yoghurt and garlic in a small bowl, then refrigerate it until you are ready to use it

3 **Soak eight wooden skewers** in cold water for 1 hour, then thread the lamb onto them and season well. Preheat the barbecue flatplate to medium–high direct heat and cook the skewers for about 3–4 minutes on each side, or until they are cooked to your liking. Serve the skewers with couscous and the yoghurt sauce.

SALMON AND PRAWN KEBABS WITH CHINESE SPICES

SERVES 4

4 x 200 g (7 oz) salmon fillets

36 raw prawns (shrimp), peeled, deveined, tails intact

5 cm (2 inch) piece fresh ginger, finely shredded

170 ml (5½ fl oz/⅔ cup) Chinese rice wine

185 ml (6 fl oz/¾ cup) kecap manis

½ teaspoon five-spice powder

200 g (7 oz) fresh egg noodles

600 g (1 lb 5 oz) baby bok choy (pak choi), leaves separated

1 **Remove skin and bones** from the salmon and cut it into bite-sized cubes (you should have about 36). Thread three cubes of salmon alternately with three prawns onto each skewer. Lay the skewers in a non-metallic dish.

2 **Combine the ginger,** rice wine, kecap manis and five-spice powder. Pour over the skewers, then cover and marinate for at least 2 hours. Turn a few times to ensure even coating.

3 **Drain, reserving the marinade.** Cook skewers in batches on a hot, lightly oiled barbecue flatplate or grill for 4–5 minutes each side, or until they are cooked through.

4 **Meanwhile, place the noodles** in a bowl and cover with boiling water. Leave for 5 minutes, or until tender, then drain and keep warm. Place the reserved marinade in a saucepan and bring to the boil. Reduce the heat, simmer and stir in the bok choy leaves. Cook, covered, for 2 minutes, or until just wilted.

5 **Top the noodles** with the bok choy, then the kebabs. Spoon on the heated marinade, season and serve.

SWEET-AND-SOUR PORK KEBABS

SERVES 6

1 kg (2 lb 4 oz) pork fillets, cubed

1 large red capsicum (pepper), cubed

1 large green capsicum (pepper), cubed

425 g (15 oz) tin pineapple pieces, drained, juice reserved

250 ml (9 fl oz/1 cup) orange juice

3 tablespoons white vinegar

2 tablespoons soft brown sugar

2 teaspoons chilli garlic sauce

2 teaspoons cornflour (cornstarch)

1 Soak six wooden skewers in water for 30 minutes to prevent scorching. Thread pieces of meat alternately with pieces of capsicum and pineapple onto the skewers. Mix the pineapple juice with the orange juice, vinegar, sugar and sauce. Place the kebabs in a shallow non-metallic dish and pour half the marinade over them. Cover and refrigerate for at least 3 hours, turning occasionally.

2 Put remaining marinade in a small saucepan. Mix the cornflour with 1 tablespoon of the marinade until smooth, then add to the pan. Stir over medium heat until the mixture boils and thickens. Transfer to a bowl, cover the surface with plastic wrap and leave to cool.

3 Cook the kebabs on a hot, lightly oiled barbecue flatplate or grill for 15 minutes, turning occasionally, until tender, and serve with the sauce.

BEEF KEBABS WITH MINT YOGHURT DRESSING

MAKES 8 KEBABS

1 kg (2 lb 4 oz) lean beef fillet, cubed

125 ml (4 fl oz/½ cup) olive oil

80 ml (2½ fl oz/⅓ cup) lemon juice

1 tablespoon chopped rosemary

2 small red onions, cut into wedges

200 g (7 oz) slender eggplants (aubergines), sliced

MINT YOGHURT DRESSING

250 g (9 oz/1 cup) plain yoghurt

1 garlic clove, crushed

1 small Lebanese (short) cucumber, grated

2 tablespoons chopped mint

1 Put the beef in a non-metallic bowl. Combine the olive oil, lemon juice and rosemary and pour over the beef. Cover and refrigerate for 2 hours.

2 To make mint yoghurt dressing, combine the yoghurt, garlic, cucumber and mint and season with salt and pepper.

3 Drain the beef and thread onto long metallic skewers, alternating pieces of beef with the onion wedges and slices of eggplant.

4 Cook the kebabs on a hot , lightly oiled barbecue grill or flatplate, turning often, for 5–10 minutes, or until the beef is cooked through and tender. Serve with the dressing.

PAPRIKA LAMB KEBABS WITH SKORDALIA

SERVES 4

1 kg (2 lb 4 oz) lamb backstraps,
   cut into 2 cm (¾ inch) cubes

1 tablespoon sweet paprika

1 tablespoon hot paprika

125 ml (4 fl oz/½ cup) lemon juice

125 ml (4 fl oz/½ cup) olive oil

3 large (750 g/1 lb 10 oz) floury potatoes
   (such as russet), cut into large cubes

3–4 garlic cloves, crushed with a pinch
   of salt

300 g (10 oz) English or baby spinach
   leaves

lemon wedges, to serve

1 **Thread six lamb cubes** onto metallic skewers and place in a non-metallic dish. Combine both of the paprikas, 80 ml (2½ fl oz/⅓ cup) of lemon juice and 60 ml (2 fl oz/¼ cup) of oil in a non-metallic jug. Pour over the skewers, turning to coat well. Season with pepper. Cover and chill while making the skordalia.

2 **Boil the potatoes** for 20 minutes, or until tender. Drain and place the potatoes, garlic and 1 tablespoon of the lemon juice in a food processor. With the motor running, slowly add the remaining oil in a thin stream and blend for 30–60 seconds, or until all the oil is incorporated — avoid overprocessing as it will become gluey. Season. Set aside to serve at room temperature.

3 **Preheat a barbecue flatplate** and brush with oil. Cook the skewers for 3–4 minutes each side for medium–rare, or 5–6 minutes for well done.

4 **Wash the spinach** and add to a saucepan with just the water clinging to the leaves. Cook, covered, over medium heat for 1–2 minutes, or until wilted. Remove from the heat and stir in the remaining lemon juice. Serve the kebabs immediately with the skordalia, spinach and lemon wedges.

TUNA SKEWERS WITH MOROCCAN SPICES

SERVES 4

800 g (1 lb 12 oz) tuna steaks,
    cut into cubes

2 tablespoons olive oil

½ teaspoon ground cumin

2 teaspoons grated lemon zest

couscous, to serve

CHERMOULA

3 teaspoons ground cumin

½ teaspoon ground coriander

2 teaspoons paprika

pinch of cayenne pepper

4 garlic cloves, crushed

3 tablespoons chopped flat-leaf
    (Italian) parsley

30 g (1 oz) chopped coriander (cilantro)
    leaves

80 ml (2½ fl oz/⅓ cup) lemon juice

125 ml (4 fl oz/½ cup) olive oil

1 **If using wooden skewers,** soak for 30 minutes beforehand to prevent scorching. Place the tuna in a shallow non-metallic dish. Combine the olive oil, ground cumin and lemon zest and pour over tuna. Toss to coat. Leave to marinate for 10 minutes.

2 **To make the chermoula,** place the cumin, coriander, paprika and cayenne in a frying pan and cook over medium heat for 30 seconds, or until fragrant. Combine with all the remaining ingredients and leave for the flavours to develop.

3 **Thread tuna** onto the skewers. Cook on a hot, lightly oiled barbecue grill or flatplate until cooked to your taste (about 1 minute on each side for rare and 2 minutes for medium). Serve on couscous with chermoula drizzled over the skewers.

LAMB KEBABS

SERVES 4

5 garlic cloves, roughly chopped

5 cm (2 inch) piece of ginger, roughly chopped

3 green chillies, roughly chopped

1 onion, roughly chopped

3 tablespoons thick natural yoghurt

3 tablespoons coriander (cilantro) leaves

½ teaspoon ground black pepper

500 g (1 lb 2 oz) minced (ground) lamb

red onion rings, to garnish

lemon wedges, to serve

1 Combine the garlic, ginger, chilli, onion, yoghurt and coriander leaves in a food processor to form a thick smooth paste. If you don't have a processor, chop the vegetables more finely and use a mortar and pestle. Add the pepper, season with salt, then mix in the mince. If you are using a mortar and pestle, mix the mince with the paste in a bowl.

2 Divide the meat into 16 portions, about 2 tablespoons each. Shape each portion into an oval patty, cover and chill for 20 minutes.

3 Using four metal skewers, thread four meatballs onto each. Cook on a hot barbecue grill or flatplate for 7 minutes, or until brown on top. Turn over and cook on the other side. Check that the meatballs are cooked. Serve with onion rings and lemon wedges.

PORK SKEWERS IN GINGER WINE AND SOY MARINADE

SERVES 4

800 g (1 lb 12 oz) pork fillets, trimmed

1 tablespoon finely grated fresh ginger

2 garlic cloves, finely chopped

1 tablespoon finely chopped preserved ginger in syrup

60 ml (2 fl oz/¼ cup) green ginger wine (see Note)

2½ tablespoons kecap manis

½ teaspoon sesame oil

1 tablespoon oil

8 spring onion bulbs, green parts removed, quartered

1 tablespoon olive oil

coriander (cilantro) sprigs, to garnish

1   **Cut the pork** into 12 cm x 2.5 cm (5 in x 1 inch) strips and put them in a non-metallic bowl with the ginger, garlic, preserved ginger, green ginger wine, kecap manis and oils, turning the meat to make sure it is evenly coated. Cover and refrigerate, leaving the meat to marinate for at least 2 hours, or overnight.

2   **Soak 12 wooden skewers** in cold water for 1 hour. Thread four pork strips into an S-shape onto each skewer. Cover skewers and refrigerate until ready to start cooking.

3   **Preheat barbecue** flatplate or grill to medium direct heat. Toss the spring onions with the olive oil and season with salt and freshly ground black pepper. Cook for 10 minutes, or until softened and well browned. When the spring onions are nearly cooked, put the kebabs on the grill plate and grill them for about 2 minutes on each side, or until pork is just cooked through and glazed. Garnish the skewers with coriander sprigs and serve immediately with the spring onion.

Note: Green ginger wine is a sweet, fortified wine with a distinctive ginger flavour. It originated in England.

TOFU KEBABS WITH MISO PESTO

SERVES 4

1 large red capsicum (pepper), cubed

12 button mushrooms, halved

6 pickling onions, quartered

3 zucchini (courgettes), cut into chunks

450 g (1 lb) firm tofu, cubed

125 ml (4 fl oz/½ cup) light olive oil

3 tablespoons light soy sauce

2 garlic cloves, crushed

2 teaspoons grated fresh ginger

MISO PESTO

90 g (3¼ oz/½ cup) unsalted roasted peanuts

60 g (2¼ oz) coriander (cilantro) leaves

2 tablespoons white miso paste

2 garlic cloves

100 ml (3½ fl oz) olive oil

1 **If using wooden skewers,** soak in water for 30 minutes to prevent scorching. Thread vegetables and tofu alternately onto 12 skewers, then place in a large non-metallic dish.

2 **Combine olive oil,** soy sauce, garlic and ginger, then pour half over the kebabs. Cover and leave to marinate for 1 hour.

3 **To make miso pesto,** finely chop the peanuts, coriander leaves, miso paste and garlic in a food processor. Slowly add the olive oil while the machine is still running and blend to a smooth paste.

4 **Cook the kebabs** on a hot, lightly oiled barbecue flatplate or grill, turning and brushing with the remaining marinade, for 4–6 minutes, or until the edges are slightly brown. Serve with the miso pesto.

INVOLTINI OF SWORDFISH

SERVES 4

1 kg (2 lb 4 oz) swordfish, skin removed, cut into four 5 cm (2 inch) pieces

3 lemons

80 ml (2½ fl oz/⅓ cup) olive oil

1 small onion, chopped

3 garlic cloves, chopped

2 tablespoons chopped capers

2 tablespoons chopped pitted Kalamata olives

35 g (1¼ oz/⅓ cup) finely grated parmesan cheese

120 g (4¼ oz/1½ cups) fresh breadcrumbs

2 tablespoons chopped parsley

1 egg, lightly beaten

24 fresh bay leaves

2 small white onions, quartered and separated into pieces

2 tablespoons lemon juice, extra

1 Cut each swordfish piece horizontally into four slices to give you 16 slices in total. Place each piece between two pieces of plastic wrap and roll gently with a rolling pin to flatten, taking care not to tear them. Cut each piece in half to give 32 pieces.

2 Peel the lemons with a vegetable peeler. Cut peel into 24 even pieces. Squeeze lemons to give 3 tablespoons of juice.

3 Heat 2 tablespoons olive oil in a pan, add the onion and garlic, and cook over medium heat for 2 minutes. Place in a bowl with the capers, olives, parmesan, breadcrumbs and parsley. Season, add the egg and mix to bind.

4 Divide the stuffing among the fish pieces and, with oiled hands, roll up to form parcels. Thread four rolls onto each of eight skewers alternating with the bay leaves, lemon peel and onion.

5 Mix the remaining oil with the lemon juice in a bowl. Cook the skewers on a hot barbecue flatplate for 3–4 minutes each side, basting with the oil and lemon mixture. Serve with a little extra lemon juice drizzled over the top.

SCALLOP AND FISH ROSEMARY SKEWERS

SERVES 4

2 tablespoons marjoram leaves

1 tablespoon lemon juice

80 ml (2½ fl oz/⅓ cup) olive oil, plus extra, for brushing

7 g (¼ cup) chopped flat-leaf (Italian) parsley

8 long firm rosemary branches

600 g (1 lb 5 oz) firm white fish fillets, cut into 3 cm (1¼ inch) cubes

16 scallops with roe attached

lemon wedges

1 **Pound marjoram leaves** in a mortar and pestle with a little salt, or very finely chop them until they become a paste. Add the lemon juice, then stir in the olive oil and parsley, and season to taste.

2 **Pull the leaves off** the rosemary branches, leaving just a tuft at the end of each stem. Thread three pieces of fish and two scallops alternately onto each rosemary skewer, brush them with a little olive oil and season well.

3 **Preheat the barbecue** flatplate to medium direct heat. Cook the skewers for 3–4 minutes on each side, or until the fish is cooked through. Serve the skewers with lemon wedges and the dressing.

SKEWERED LAMB WITH CHILLI AÏOLI

MAKES 12 SKEWERS

1.5 kg (3 lb 5 oz) leg of lamb, boned
    and cubed

125 ml (4 fl oz/½ cup) olive oil

125 ml (4 fl oz/½ cup) lemon juice

2 garlic cloves, crushed

1 teaspoon cracked black pepper

1 tablespoon Dijon mustard

1 tablespoon chopped oregano

CHILLI AÏOLI

2–3 small red chillies, seeded

3 garlic cloves

½ teaspoon ground black pepper

3 egg yolks

2 tablespoons lemon juice

200 ml (7 fl oz) olive oil

1 **Put the lamb** in a large, non-metallic bowl. Add combined olive oil, lemon juice, garlic, pepper, mustard and oregano. Toss well, cover and refrigerate for at least 3 hours.

2 **Soak 12 wooden skewers** in water to prevent scorching. Drain the lamb, reserving the marinade. Thread lamb onto the skewers. Cook on a hot, lightly oiled barbecue grill or flatplate until well browned, brushing with the marinade a few times.

3 **To make the chilli aïoli,** chop the chillies and garlic for 30 seconds in a food processor. Add the pepper, egg yolks and 2 teaspoons of lemon juice. With the motor running, slowly pour in the oil in a fine stream. Increase the flow as the aïoli thickens. Add the remaining lemon juice and season to taste. Serve with the skewered lamb.

MUSHROOM AND EGGPLANT SKEWERS

SERVES 4

12 long rosemary sprigs

18 Swiss brown mushrooms, halved

1 small eggplant (aubergine), cubed

60 ml (2 fl oz/¼ cup) olive oil

2 tablespoons balsamic vinegar

2 garlic cloves, crushed

1 teaspoon sugar

TOMATO SAUCE

5 tomatoes

1 tablespoon olive oil

1 small onion, finely chopped

1 garlic clove, crushed

1 tablespoon tomato paste (purée)

2 teaspoons sugar

2 teaspoons balsamic vinegar

1 tablespoon chopped flat-leaf
   (Italian) parsley

1 Remove the leaves from the lower part of the rosemary sprigs. Reserve 1 tablespoon of the leaves. Put mushrooms and eggplant in a large non-metallic bowl. Pour on combined oil, vinegar, garlic and sugar and toss. Marinate for 15 minutes.

2 To make the tomato sauce, score a cross in the base of each tomato. Put in a bowl of boiling water for 30 seconds, then plunge into cold water. Peel the skin away from the cross. Cut in half and scoop out seeds with a teaspoon. Dice flesh.

3 Heat the oil in a saucepan. Cook the onion and garlic over medium heat for 2–3 minutes, or until soft. Reduce the heat, add the tomato, tomato paste, sugar, vinegar and parsley and simmer for 10 minutes, or until thick.

4 Carefully thread mushroom halves and eggplant cubes alternately onto the rosemary sprigs. Cook on a hot, lightly oiled barbecue grill or flat plate for 7–8 minutes, or until the eggplant is tender, turning occasionally. Serve with the sauce.

VEGETARIAN SKEWERS WITH BASIL COUSCOUS

SERVES 4

5 thin zucchini (courgettes), cut into
   2 cm (¾ inch) cubes

5 slender eggplants (aubergines), cut
   into 2 cm (¾ inch) cubes

12 button mushrooms, halved

2 red capsicums (peppers), cut into
   2 cm (¾ inch) cubes

250 g (9 oz) kefalotyri cheese, cut into
   2 cm (¾ inch) thick pieces

80 ml (2½ fl oz/⅓ cup) lemon juice

2 garlic cloves, finely chopped

5 tablespoons finely chopped basil

145 ml (5 fl oz) extra virgin olive oil

185 g (6½ oz/1 cup) couscous

1 teaspoon grated lemon zest

lemon wedges, to serve

1 Using 12 metallic skewers, thread alternate pieces of vegetables and kefalotyri, starting and finishing with capsicum and using two pieces of kefalotyri per skewer. Place in a large non-metallic dish. Combine lemon juice, garlic, 4 tablespoons of basil and 125 ml (4 fl oz/½ cup) of oil in a non-metallic bowl. Season well. Pour two-thirds of the marinade over the skewers, reserving the remainder. Turn the skewers to coat evenly, cover with plastic wrap and marinate for at least 10 minutes in a cool place.

2 Put the couscous, zest and 375 ml (13 fl oz/1½ cups) boiling water in a large heatproof bowl. Stand for 5 minutes, or until the water has been absorbed. Add the remaining oil and basil, then fluff with a fork to separate the grains.

3 Meanwhile, heat a barbecue flatplate to medium–high. Cook the skewers, brushing often with the leftover marinade, for 4–5 minutes each side, or until the vegetables are cooked and the cheese browns.

4 Divide the couscous and skewers among four serving plates. Season, then drizzle with the reserved marinade. Serve immediately with lemon wedges.

CHORIZO AND HALOUMI SKEWERS

SERVES 4

2 chorizo sausages (see Note)

2 x 180 g (6 oz) packet haloumi cheese

1 lemon

LEMON AND MINT DRESSING

1 tablespoon lemon juice

2 tablespoons extra virgin olive oil

1 tablespoon finely chopped mint

½ teaspoon finely grated lemon zest

1 Soak 12 bamboo skewers in cold water for 30 minutes. Preheat a barbecue grill plate or flatplate to medium.

2 Chop the chorizo and haloumi into bite-sized pieces. Cut the lemon into 12 wedges, then slice each wedge in half. Thread the chorizo, haloumi and lemon pieces alternately onto the soaked bamboo skewers.

3 In a small bowl, whisk all the lemon and mint dressing ingredients together, then season to taste and set aside.

4 Brush the flatplate with a little oil, add the skewers and cook for a few minutes on each side, or until the chorizo is cooked through and the skewers are golden brown all over. Spoon the dressing over the hot skewers and serve at once.

Note: Chorizo sausages are made from highly seasoned minced (ground) pork and are flavoured with garlic, chilli and a number of other spices. They come in fresh and cured versions. Either type can be used here. They're available from delicatessens, specialty butchers and some supermarkets,

SATAY CHICKEN SKEWERS

SERVES 4

500 g (1 lb 2 oz) chicken thigh fillets, cut into 1 cm (½ inch) wide strips

1 garlic clove, crushed

2 teaspoons finely grated fresh ginger

3 teaspoons fish sauce

SATAY SAUCE

2 teaspoons peanut oil

4 red Asian shallots, finely chopped

4 garlic cloves, crushed

2 teaspoons finely chopped fresh ginger

2 small red chillies, seeded and finely chopped

125 g (4½ oz/½ cup) crunchy peanut butter

185 ml (6 fl oz/¾ cup) coconut milk

2 teaspoons soy sauce

2 teaspoons grated palm sugar or soft brown sugar

1½ tablespoons fish sauce

1 fresh kaffir (makrut) lime leaf

1½ tablespoons lime juice

1 Put the chicken, garlic, ginger and fish sauce in a bowl and turn the chicken so that it is well coated. Cover the bowl and leave it in the refrigerator for 1 hour.

2 Soak 12 wooden skewers in cold water for 1 hour.

3 To make the satay sauce, heat the oil in a saucepan over medium heat, then add the shallot, garlic, ginger and chilli. Stir mixture constantly with a wooden spoon for 5 minutes, or until the shallots are golden. Reduce heat to low, add the remaining sauce ingredients and simmer for 10 minutes, or until the sauce has thickened. Remove the lime leaf and keep the sauce warm while you cook the chicken.

4 Preheat the barbecue grill to medium–high direct heat. Thread two or three chicken strips onto each skewer, without crowding them, and grill the chicken for 10 minutes, or until it is cooked through, turning after 5 minutes. Serve the skewers with the satay sauce.

BEEF SATAY SKEWERS

SERVES 4

650 g (1 lb 7 oz) rump steak, finely sliced

lime wedges, to serve

2 tablespoons chopped coriander (cilantro) leaves, to serve

SATAY SAUCE

2 teaspoons peanut oil

1 small onion, finely chopped

2 tablespoons chopped lemon grass, white part only

2 tablespoons finely grated fresh ginger or galangal

1 red bird's eye chilli, finely chopped

140 g (5 oz) crunchy peanut butter

250 ml (9 fl oz/1 cup) coconut milk

1 Soak 12 bamboo skewers in cold water for 20 minutes. Thread the beef evenly onto the skewers.

2 To make the satay sauce, heat the oil in a small saucepan over medium heat and cook the onion, stirring, for 3 minutes, or until soft. Add the lemongrass, ginger and chilli and cook, stirring, for 1 minute, or until fragrant. Stir in the peanut butter and coconut milk and cook over low heat until well combined and heated through.

3 Heat an oiled barbecue grill to high heat. Lightly brush the beef with oil. Cook the skewers for about 3 minutes on each side, or until browned and cooked as desired.

4 Serve the beef with the satay sauce and lime wedges and sprinkle with the coriander.

TANDOORI-STYLE PRAWNS

SERVES 6

¾ teaspoon saffron threads

1 small onion, quartered

3 garlic cloves, peeled

2 teaspoons grated fresh ginger

2 tablespoons lemon juice

½ teaspoon chilli powder

1 teaspoon paprika

pinch of ground coriander

pinch of ground cumin

2 teaspoons garam masala

1–2 drops red food colouring for colour (optional)

1 tablespoon oil

1 teaspoon salt

200 g (7 oz) Greek-style yoghurt

30 prawns (shrimp), peeled and deveined, tails intact

lemon wedges and naan bread, to serve

1 **Soak the saffron** in 1 tablespoon hot water for 5 minutes. Add the saffron and its soaking liquid to a food processor with the onion, garlic, ginger, lemon juice, chilli powder, paprika, coriander, cumin, garam masala, food colouring, oil and salt. Process to a paste. Scoop into a bowl. Stir in the yoghurt.

2 **Thread five prawns** onto each of six metal skewers (if you're using bamboo skewers, soak them in water for 30 minutes first). Put in a non-metallic ovenproof dish (pick one that will fit in your oven) and cover with the marinade. Cover with plastic wrap and refrigerate for 2–3 hours. Allow the prawns to come to room temperature.

3 **Cook the skewers** on a hot barbecue flatplate under a hot griller (broiler) for 2 minutes on each side, or until lightly browned and the marinade has dried up. Serve with lemon wedges and naan bread.

ROSEMARY TUNA KEBABS

SERVES 4

3 tomatoes

1 tablespoon olive oil

2–3 small red chillies, deseeded and chopped

3–4 garlic cloves, crushed

1 red onion, finely chopped

60 ml (2 fl oz/¼ cup) white wine or water

400 g (14 oz) tinned chickpeas

3 tablespoons chopped oregano

4 tablespoons chopped parsley

lemon wedges, to serve

TUNA KEBABS

1 kg (2 lb 4 oz) piece of tuna, cut into 4 cm (1½ in) cubes

8 stems of rosemary, about 20 cm (8 inches) long, with the leaves from the stem thinned out a little

1 Cut the tomatoes into halves or quarters and use a teaspoon to scrape out the seeds. Roughly chop the flesh.

2 Heat the oil in a large non-stick frying pan. Add chilli, garlic and red onion and stir over medium heat for 5 minutes, or until softened. Add chopped tomato and the white wine or water. Cook over low heat for 10 minutes, or until the mixture is soft and pulpy and most of the liquid has evaporated. Stir in the rinsed chickpeas with the oregano and parsley. Season to taste with salt and freshly ground black pepper.

3 Heat barbecue flatplate to medium–high heat. Thread tuna onto the rosemary stems, lightly spray with oil, then cook, turning, for 3 minutes, or until lightly browned on the outside but still a little pink in the centre. Serve with the chickpeas and some lemon wedges.

SWORDFISH SHISH KEBABS WITH HERB YOGHURT

SERVES 4

800 g (1 lb 12 oz) skinless swordfish
   fillet, cut into 3 cm (1¼ inch) chunks

80 ml (2½ fl oz/⅓ cup) lemon juice

80 ml (2½ fl oz/⅓ cup) olive oil

3 bay leaves

16 whole cherry tomatoes or 2 firm
   tomatoes, each cut into 8 wedges

2 small red onions, each cut into
   8 wedges

2 small red or orange capsicums
   (peppers), each deseeded and cut
   into 8 even chunks

LEMON AND HERB YOGHURT

200 g (7 oz) Greek-style yoghurt

3 teaspoons lemon juice

pinch of paprika

1 tablespoon finely chopped mint

1 tablespoon finely chopped parsley

COUSCOUS

400 g (14 oz) instant couscous

400 ml (14 fl oz) boiling stock

1 tablespoon olive oil

30 g (1 oz) butter

1 Put the chunks of swordfish in a non-metallic bowl with the lemon juice, olive oil and bay leaves. Toss to mix, cover and leave to marinate for at least 2 hours in the fridge.

2 If using bamboo skewers, first soak them in water for 30 minutes to prevent scorching. You will need eight skewers.

3 In a small bowl, whisk together the ingredients for the lemon and herb yoghurt. Refrigerate until needed.

4 Thread five pieces of fish, two cherry tomatoes, two pieces of onion and two pieces of capsicum onto a skewer, alternating between the fish and various vegetables as you go.

5 Cook the kebabs on a barbecue flatplate for 8–10 minutes. Baste with remaining marinade as they cook, and turn every now and then. When ready, the fish should be firm and look opaque and the vegetables should be slightly charred.

6 Meanwhile, tip the couscous into a heatproof bowl, pour on the stock and oil, cover tightly and leave to sit for 5 minutes. Fluff the grains with a fork and stir in the butter.

7 Serve the kebabs on a mound of couscous, drizzled with some of the yoghurt dressing

HONEY AND LIME PRAWN KEBABS WITH SALSA

SERVES 4

32 prawns (shrimp), peeled and deveined, tails intact

3 tablespoons clear runny honey

1 small red chilli, deseeded and finely chopped

2 tablespoons olive oil

zest and juice of 2 limes

1 large garlic clove, crushed

2 cm (¾ inch) piece of fresh ginger, finely grated

1 tablespoon chopped coriander (cilantro) leaves

SALSA

2 tomatoes

1 small just-ripe mango, diced

½ small red onion, diced

1 small red chilli, deseeded and finely chopped

zest and juice of 1 lime

2 tablespoons chopped coriander (cilantro) leaves

1 **Put the prawns in a non-metallic dish.** Whisk the honey, chilli, olive oil, lime zest and juice, garlic, ginger and coriander together, then pour over the prawns. Toss well. Cover and marinate in the fridge for at least 3 hours, turning occasionally.

2 **Meanwhile, soak eight bamboo** skewers in water for 30 minutes. This is to ensure they don't burn during cooking.

3 **For the salsa,** score a cross in the base of each tomato. Cover with boiling water for 30 seconds, then plunge into cold water. Peel the skin away from the cross. Dice the tomatoes, discarding the cores and saving any juice. In a bowl, mix the tomatoes and juice with the mango, red onion, chilli, lime zest and juice and coriander.

4 **Preheat the barbecue** flatplate to high. Thread four prawns onto each skewer. Cook for 4 minutes, turning halfway through cooking. Baste regularly with the leftover marinade as they cook. The prawns will turn pink and be lightly browned on both sides. Serve the kebabs with the salsa and some rice.

SPICY SAUSAGES WITH HARISSA AND COUSCOUS

SERVES 4

2 tablespoons butter

300 g (11 oz/1½ cups) instant couscous

2 teaspoons harissa

60 ml (2 fl oz/¼ cup) olive oil

2 tablespoons lemon juice

1½ tablespoons grated lemon zest

2 tablespoons parsley, chopped

150 g (5½ oz) chargrilled red capsicum (pepper), sliced

40 g (1½ oz/⅓ cup) raisins

12 merguez sausages

thick plain yoghurt, to serve

1 **Put the butter** in a saucepan with 500 ml (17 fl oz/2 cups) water and bring to the boil. Sprinkle in the couscous, mix it into the water, then take it off the stove. Put a lid on the pan and leave it to sit for 5 minutes. Stir the harissa, olive oil, lemon juice and zest together until well mixed. Add the parsley, red capsicum and raisins and leave everything to marinate briefly.

2 **Cook the sausages** on a barbecue flatplate or grill for 8 minutes, turning them so they brown on all sides.

3 **Meanwhile,** remove the lid from the couscous, stir for a minute or two to separate the grains, then gently stir in the harissa mixture.

4 **Serve the couscous** with the sausages sliced over it and topped with a large dollop of yoghurt.

TURMERIC FISHCAKES ON LEMON GRASS SKEWERS

MAKES 15

6 large red chillies, deseeded and chopped
6 garlic cloves, chopped
4 red Asian shallots, chopped
50 g (1¾ oz) fresh turmeric, peeled and roughly chopped
50 g (1¾ oz) piece fresh ginger, peeled and chopped
50 g (1¾ oz/⅓ cup) unsalted peanuts
1 tomato, halved and deseeded
2 teaspoons ground coriander
125 ml (4 fl oz/½ cup) peanut oil
2 tablespoons grated palm sugar (jaggery) or soft brown sugar
500 g (1 lb 2 oz) boneless snapper fillet, roughly chopped
4 makrut (kaffir lime) leaves, spines removed, chopped
15 lemon grass stems
sweet chilli sauce, to serve

1 **Put the chillies,** garlic, shallots, turmeric, ginger, peanuts, tomato, coriander and 125 ml (4 fl oz/½ cup) of water in a food processor and blend to form a coarse paste. Spoon into a heavy-based saucepan and add the oil and palm sugar. Simmer over medium heat for 15–18 minutes, or until the water has evaporated and the paste is a rich golden colour. Set aside to cool completely.

2 **Put fish pieces,** lime leaves, salt and pepper and 125 ml (4 fl oz/½ cup) of the turmeric spice paste into the bowl of a food processor. Blend for 1–2 minutes, or until the fish is finely chopped and the mixture is well combined.

3 **Trim each piece of lemon grass** to form a 20 cm (8 inch) stick. Mould a heaped tablespoon of the fish mixture around each piece of lemon grass at one end. Cook on a lightly greased preheated barbecue grill for 3 minutes on each side, or until golden brown. Serve immediately with sweet chilli sauce.

SPANISH-STYLE BEEF KEBABS

MAKES 18–20

1 kg (2 lb 4 oz) rump steak

3 garlic cloves, chopped

1 tablespoon chopped flat-leaf (Italian) parsley

80 ml (2½ fl oz/⅓ cup) lemon juice

lemon wedges, to serve

PAPRIKA DRESSING

2 teaspoons paprika

large pinch cayenne pepper

2 tablespoons red wine vinegar

80 ml (2½ fl oz/⅓ cup) olive oil

½ teaspoon salt

1 **Trim any excess fat** from the beef and cut into 2 cm (¾ inch) pieces. Combine the beef, garlic, parsley, lemon juice and ½ teaspoon pepper in a non-metallic bowl, cover with plastic wrap and marinate in the refrigerator for 2 hours. Meanwhile, soak 20 wooden skewers in water for 30 minutes to ensure they don't burn during cooking.

2 **To make the paprika dressing,** whisk paprika, cayenne pepper, vinegar, oil and salt together until well blended.

3 **Heat a lightly oiled** barbecue flatplate. Thread the pieces of marinated beef onto the skewers, then cook the kebabs, turning occasionally, for 4–5 minutes, or until cooked through. Drizzle with paprika dressing. Serve hot with lemon wedges.

TERYAKI STEAK KEBABS

750 g (1 lb 10 oz) lean rump steak

125 ml (4 fl oz/½ cup) soy sauce

125 ml (4 fl oz/½ cup) sherry or sake

1 garlic clove, crushed

1 teaspoon ground ginger

1 teaspoon sugar

lime wedges, to serve

1 Cut the steak into thin strips, 15 cm (6 inch) long and thread the slices onto 24 wooden skewers.

2 Combine the soy sauce, sherry or sake, garlic and ground ginger and sugar.

3 Put the steak in a shallow non-metallic dish and marinate in the soy sauce mixture for at least 1 hour in the refrigerator, then drain.

4 Cook the skewers on a preheated barbecue flatplate for 3–4 minutes each side, or until cooked to your liking. Serve with lime wedges.

CHILLI PRAWN SKEWERS

MAKES 30

30 large raw prawns (shrimp)

60 g (2¼ oz) butter

1 garlic clove, crushed

2 teaspoons soft brown sugar

2 tablespoons lemon or lime juice

2 tablespoons finely chopped coriander (cilantro) sprigs

2 tablespoons finely chopped basil leaves

1 tablespoon sweet chilli sauce

1 **Peel the prawns,** leaving the tails intact. Gently pull out the dark vein from each prawn back, starting from the head end.

2 **Heat the butter** in a large frying pan over medium heat. Add the garlic, sugar, juice, coriander, basil and sweet chilli sauce. Mix thoroughly.

3 **Put the prawns** on a medium barbecue flatplate and pour over the butter mixture. Cook, turning often, for 5 minutes or until the prawns turn pink and are cooked through.

4 **Thread each prawn** onto a bamboo skewer or strong toothpick to serve.

Note: Prepare the prawns several hours ahead. Cook just before serving. Scallops or oysters can be used instead of prawns, or alternate pieces of fish with prawns.

CHILLI PORK KEBABS

MAKES 8

500 g (1 lb 2 oz) pork fillet

2 tablespoons sweet chilli sauce

2 tablespoons tomato sauce (ketchup)

2 tablespoons hoisin sauce

2 garlic cloves, crushed

60 ml (2 fl oz/¼ cup) lemon juice

2 tablespoons honey

2 teaspoons grated fresh ginger

ready-made satay sauce, to serve

1 **Trim the fat and sinew** from the pork, cut meat into small cubes and place in a non-metallic bowl.

2 **Combine the sweet chilli sauce,** tomato sauce, hoisin sauce, garlic, lemon juice, honey and ginger. Pour over the pork and stir well. Cover and refrigerate for several hours, or overnight.

3 **Soak 8 wooden skewers** in water for 30 minutes to ensure they don't burn during cooking. Thread the pork onto the skewers.

4 **Heat a little oil** on a barbecue flatplate and cook the skewers for 3–4 minutes each side, or until cooked through. Brush with the remaining marinade while cooking. Serve with satay sauce.

GARLIC LAMB SKEWERS

MAKES 35

600 g (1 lb 5 oz) trimmed lamb steaks

1 garlic bulb

1 red chilli, chopped

2 garlic cloves, crushed

3 tablespoons oil

1 **Cut the lamb steaks** into 2 cm (¾ inch) cubes and halve each garlic clove lengthways.

2 **Thread 2 pieces of lamb** and 2 slices of garlic alternately onto 35 small metal skewers.

3 **Combine the chilli,** crushed garlic cloves and oil.

4 **Heat a barbecue grill** to medium–high and lightly brush with oil. Cook the skewers for 2–5 minutes, brushing occasionally with the garlic and chilli marinade.

TANDOORI CHICKEN WITH CARDAMOM RICE

SERVES 4

250 ml (9 fl oz/1 cup) natural yoghurt, plus extra for serving

60 g (2 oz/¼ cup) tandoori paste

2 tablespoons lemon juice

1 kg (2 lb 4 oz) boneless, skinless chicken breast, cut into 4 cm (1½ inch) cubes

1 tablespoon oil

1 onion, finely diced

300 g (11 oz/1½ cups) long-grain rice

2 cardamom pods, bruised

750 ml (13 fl oz/3 cups) hot chicken stock

400 g (14 oz) English or baby spinach leaves

1 Soak eight wooden skewers in water for 30 minutes to prevent them burning during cooking. Combine the yoghurt, tandoori paste and lemon juice in a non-metallic dish. Add the chicken and coat well with the mixture. Cover and marinate for at least 15 minutes.

2 Meanwhile, heat the oil in a saucepan. Add the onion and cook for 3 minutes, then add the rice and cardamom pods. Cook, stirring often, for 3–5 minutes, or until the rice is slightly opaque. Add the hot chicken stock and bring to the boil. Reduce the heat to low, cover, and cook the rice, without removing the lid, for 15 minutes.

3 Heat a barbecue plate or oven grill (broiler) to very hot. Thread chicken cubes onto the skewers, leaving the bottom quarter of the skewers empty. Cook on each side for about 5 minutes, or until cooked through.

4 Wash the spinach and put in a large saucepan with just the water clinging to the leaves. Cook, covered, over medium heat for 1–2 minutes, or until the spinach has wilted. Uncover rice, fluff up with a fork and serve with the spinach, chicken and extra yoghurt.

LAMB SAUSAGES WITH CAPSICUM AND ONION

SERVES 4

8 merguez or other spicy sausages

1 green capsicum (pepper)

1 red capsicum (pepper)

1 large brown onion

2 tablespoons olive oil

2 rounds of Moroccan bread or pitta breads, to serve

1 **Prick sausages with a fork,** then cook on a barbecue grill over low–medium heat, turning frequently, for 8–10 minutes, or until cooked through.

2 **Meanwhile, cut the capsicums** into quarters, remove the seeds and white membrane and cut into strips about 1 cm (½ inch) wide. Halve the onion and slice thinly. Heat the olive oil in a frying pan on the barbecue, add the capsicum strips and onion and cook over medium heat, stirring often, for about 10 minutes, or until tender. If the onion begins to burn, reduce heat to low or move the pan to a cooler section of the barbecue. Season with salt and freshly ground black pepper.

3 **If serving with Moroccan bread,** cut the rounds into quarters. Place the sausages and a generous amount of the capsicum and onion mixture in the bread, or roll up in pitta bread. Alternatively, serve the sausages on plates with the vegetables, and the bread on the side.

FENNEL AND PORK SAUSAGES WITH ONION RELISH

MAKES 8

750 g (1 lb 10 oz) minced (ground) pork

40 g (1½ oz/½ cup) fresh breadcrumbs

2 garlic cloves, crushed

3 teaspoons fennel seeds, coarsely crushed

1 teaspoon finely grated orange zest

2 teaspoons chopped thyme leaves

7 g (¼ oz) chopped flat-leaf (Italian) parsley

oil, for brushing

1 long baguette, cut into 4 pieces, or 4 long, crusty rolls

50 g (1¾ oz) butter, softened

60 g (2¼ oz) rocket (arugula) leaves

1 tablespoon extra virgin olive oil

1 teaspoon balsamic vinegar

ONION RELISH

50 g (1¾ oz) butter

2 red onions, thinly sliced

1 tablespoon soft brown sugar

2 tablespoons balsamic vinegar

1 Put the pork, breadcrumbs, garlic, fennel seeds, zest, thyme and parsley in a large bowl, season well with salt and freshly ground black pepper and mix everything together with your hands. Cover the mixture and refrigerate it for 4 hours or overnight.

2 To make the onion relish, melt the butter in a heavy-based saucepan, add the onion and cook, stirring occasionally, over low heat for about 10 minutes, or until the onion is softened, but not browned. Add the sugar and vinegar, and continue to cook for another 30 minutes, stirring regularly.

3 Preheat a barbecue flatplate to medium direct heat. Divide the pork mixture into eight portions and use wet hands to mould each portion into a flattish sausage shape. Lightly brush the sausages with oil and cook them for 8 minutes on each side, or until they are cooked through.

4 To assemble, split the rolls down the middle and butter them. Toss the rocket with the olive oil and balsamic vinegar, and put some of the leaves in each of the rolls. Top with a sausage and some of the onion relish.

CHIPOLATAS WITH JALAPEÑO QUESADILLAS

SERVES 4

2 tablespoons olive oil

2 garlic cloves, crushed

2 x 400 g (14 oz) tin crushed tomatoes

½ teaspoon ground cumin

16 x 15 cm (6 in) flour tortillas

320 g (11½ oz) coarsely grated cheddar
cheese

60 g (2¼ oz/⅓ cup) pickled jalapeño
chillies, drained and roughly chopped

20 spicy chipolatas

coriander (cilantro) sprigs, to garnish

1 **Heat the olive oil** in a frying pan over medium heat and cook the garlic for 1–2 minutes or until it is just beginning to turn golden. Add the crushed tomatoes and cumin, and season well. Reduce the heat to low and cook the relish for 30–35 minutes or until it becomes thick and pulpy.

2 **In the meantime,** sprinkle a tortilla with 40 g (1½ oz/ ⅓ cup) of the grated cheese, leaving a 1 cm (½ inch) border around the edge. Scatter 1½ teaspoons of jalapeño chillies over the cheese and put another tortilla on top, pressing it down. Repeat the process with remaining tortillas, cheese and jalapeños to make eight quesadillas.

3 **Preheat the barbecue** to low direct heat. Cook the chipolatas on the flatplate, turning them occasionally, for 10–12 minutes or until they are cooked through. When the chipolatas are nearly ready, start cooking the quesadillas on the grill for 1–2 minutes on each side, or until the cheese has melted. You may need to do this in batches, so make sure you keep them warm as you go.

4 **Cut each quesadilla** into quarters and serve with the tomato relish and chipolatas. Garnish with the coriander.

CHIPOLATAS WITH SAGE AND PANCETTA

SERVES 4

16 chipolata sausages

16 sage leaves

8 thin slices pancetta, cut in half

oil, for brushing

FRESH TOMATO SALSA

4 roma (plum) tomatoes, cut into 1 cm (½ inch) cubes

1 tablespoon extra virgin olive oil

1 teaspoon balsamic vinegar

1 garlic clove, very thinly sliced

1 tablespoon chopped mint leaves

1 teaspoon chopped sage leaves

1 Soak eight bamboo skewers in cold water for 30 minutes. Meanwhile, put the chipolatas in a saucepan and cover with cold water. Bring to the boil, remove from the heat and drain well. (Parboiling the chipolatas will help them cook evenly.)

2 Preheat a barbecue grill or flatplate to low. Put a sage leaf along a chipolata and wrap half a slice of pancetta around it, to almost cover the chipolata. Repeat with the remaining sausages.

3 Thread 4 chipolatas onto a skewer about a quarter of the way in from one end of the sausages, so they poke out in the same direction like four little flags. Now push a second skewer up through the other end of the chipolatas so that they are suspended between two skewers. Repeat with the remaining sausages.

4 Lightly brush the flatplate with oil and cook chipolatas for about 8 minutes, or until browned on both sides and cooked through, turning once — keep an eye on the pancetta to make sure it doesn't burn.

5 Meanwhile, put all the tomato salsa ingredients together in a bowl, season with salt and freshly ground black pepper and mix together well. Arrange the skewers on a serving plate, spoon some salsa over the top and serve at once.

SAUSAGES AND MASH WITH FRENCH SHALLOT GRAVY

SERVES 4

80 ml (2½ fl oz/⅓ cup) olive oil

200 g (7 oz) French shallots, thinly sliced

1 tablespoon plain (all-purpose) flour

125 ml (4 fl oz/½ cup) red wine

375 ml (13 fl oz/1½ cups) beef stock

1 tablespoon Dijon mustard

1.5 kg (3 lb 5 oz) potatoes, chopped

150 g (5½ oz) butter

8 thick pork sausages (about 100 g/
3½ oz each)

450 g (1 lb) green beans, topped and
tailed

1 Heat 2 **tablespoons oil** in a large frying pan over medium heat. Add the French shallots and cook for 5 minutes, stirring often until they soften. Add the flour and cook for 30 seconds. Increase the heat, pour in the wine and stock and bring to the boil. Reduce the heat and simmer for 10 minutes, or until the gravy thickens. Stir in the mustard, then reduce the heat to medium–low and simmer gently until the sausages and mash are ready.

2 Cook the **potatoes** in boiling water until tender. Drain, return to the pan and add 1 tablespoon olive oil and 120 g (4 oz) butter. Mash until smooth, then season with salt and black pepper.

3 While the **potatoes** are cooking, prick the sausages with a fork. Heat a barbecue hotplate to medium, add the remaining oil and the sausages. Cook for 10 minutes, or until cooked through, turning often.

4 Bring a **saucepan** of lightly salted water to the boil, add beans and cook for 4 minutes, or until just tender. Whisk the remaining butter into the gravy and season. Place a mound of mash on each plate, top with the sausages and gravy, and serve with the beans on the side.

SPLIT SAUSAGES WITH CARAMELIZED ONIONS

SERVES 4

CARAMELIZED ONIONS

1 tablespoon olive oil

1 tablespoon butter

3 large red onions, thinly sliced

1 teaspoon thyme leaves, chopped

1 tablespoon balsamic vinegar

8 thick beef sausages

150 g (5½ oz) gorgonzola cheese, crumbled

8 thyme sprigs

1 **To make caramelized onions,** heat the olive oil and butter in a saucepan, add the onion and stir over medium heat until the onion is well coated. Cook for 5 minutes, or until the onion starts to soften. Add thyme, put the lid on and turn the heat to low. Cook for 40 minutes, stirring from time to time, until the onion becomes a deep, rich, golden brown. Add vinegar and cook for another minute.

2 **Meanwhile, heat the barbecue** flatplate to high. Cook the sausages for 5–10 minutes, turning them from time to time to ensure they brown all over.

3 **Remove sausages** from the heat and split them down the middle, being careful not to cut all the way through. Fill them with the caramelized onion, sprinkle the crumbled gorgonzola over the top, then grill (broil) for 1 minute, or until the cheese has melted. Served warm, garnished with thyme sprigs. These are excellent with a green leaf salad and baked jacket potatoes dolloped with some sour cream mixed with seeded mustard.

BURGERS & PATTIES

BEEF AND MOZZARELLA BURGERS

SERVES 4

500 g (1 lb 2 oz) minced (ground) beef

160 g (5¾ oz/2 cups) fresh breadcrumbs

1 small red onion, very finely chopped

4 garlic cloves, crushed

30 g (1 oz) finely shredded basil leaves

50 g (1¾ oz) pitted black olives, finely chopped

1 tablespoon balsamic vinegar

1 egg

8 pieces mozzarella 2 cm x 3 cm x 5 mm (¾ x 1¼ x ¼ inch)

CHARGRILLED TOMATOES

6 roma (plum) tomatoes

1½ tablespoons olive oil

1 Put the beef, breadcrumbs, onion, garlic, basil, olives, balsamic vinegar and egg in a large bowl and season well with salt and pepper. Use your hands to mix everything together, then cover and refrigerate the mixture for about 2 hours.

2 Divide the beef mixture into eight portions and roll each portion into a ball. Push a piece of mozzarella into the middle of each ball, then push the mince mixture over to cover the hole and flatten the ball to form a patty.

3 To make the chargrilled tomatoes, slice the tomatoes in half lengthways and toss them with the olive oil. Spray the flatplate with olive oil and preheat it to high direct heat. Cook the tomatoes, cut-side down, for 8 minutes then turn them over and cook for another 5 minutes or until they are soft.

4 Cook the patties on one side for 5 minutes then flip and cook for another 5 minutes or until they are completely cooked through and the cheese has melted. Serve the burgers and chargrilled tomatoes with a fresh green salad.

STEAK SANDWICH WITH BALSAMIC ONIONS

SERVES 4

125 g (4½ oz/½ cup) sour cream

40 g (1½ oz) sun-dried tomatoes, well drained and finely chopped

3 garlic cloves, crushed

2 tablespoons finely chopped basil leaves

2 teaspoons lemon juice

2 red onions

2 tablespoons olive oil

2 tablespoons balsamic vinegar

1 tablespoon soft brown sugar

8 large slices of sourdough bread

400 g (14 oz) piece of fillet steak, cut into 1 cm (½ inch) thick slices

55 g (2 oz) baby rocket (arugula) leaves, rinsed and well drained

1 **Preheat the barbecue** flatplate or grill to medium–high direct heat. Mix the sour cream, sun-dried tomatoes, garlic, basil and lemon juice in a small bowl and season the mixture to taste.

2 **Thinly slice the onions,** separate the rings and toss them with 1 tablespoon of olive oil. Spread the onion across the flat plate and cook it for 10 minutes, or until softened and starting to brown. Gather the rings into a pile and pour the combined balsamic vinegar and sugar over them. Turn the onion so that it is well coated in the balsamic mixture, then spread it out a little and cook for a few more minutes, or until it is slightly glazed. Remove the onion from the barbecue and toast the bread on the grill for 30 seconds on each side, or until grill marks appear.

3 **Brush the steaks** with a little olive oil and season with salt and ground black pepper. Cook for 1 minute each side for medium–rare, or 2 minutes for well done.

4 **To serve, put a piece of steak** on a slice of toasted bread and top with the onion, a dollop of the sour cream mixture and some rocket leaves. Finish with a second piece of toast.

BRUNCH BURGER WITH THE WORKS

SERVES 6

750 g (1 lb 10 oz) minced (ground) beef

1 onion, finely chopped

1 egg

40 g (1½ oz/½ cup) fresh breadcrumbs

2 tablespoons tomato paste
(condensed purée)

1 tablespoon Worcestershire sauce

2 tablespoons chopped flat-leaf
(Italian) parsley

3 large onions

30 g (1 oz) butter

6 cheddar cheese slices

butter, extra, for cooking

6 eggs, extra

6 bacon rashers

6 large hamburger buns, lightly toasted

shredded lettuce

2 tomatoes, thinly sliced

6 large slices beetroot, drained

6 pineapple rings, drained

tomato sauce, to serve

1 **Combine the beef,** onion, egg, breadcrumbs, tomato paste, Worcestershire sauce and parsley with your hands. Season well. Divide into six portions and shape into burgers. Cover and set aside.

2 **Slice onions into thin rings.** Heat butter on a barbecue flatplate. Cook the onion, turning often, until well browned. Move the onion to the outer edge of the flatplate to keep warm. Brush the barbecue grill or flatplate liberally with oil.

3 **Cook the burgers** for 3–4 minutes each side, or until browned and cooked through. Move to the cooler part of the barbecue or transfer to a plate and keep warm. Place a slice of cheese on each burger.

4 **Heat a small amount** of butter on a barbecue flat plate or in a large frying pan. Fry the eggs and bacon until the eggs are cooked through and the bacon is golden and crisp. Fill the hamburger buns with lettuce, tomato, beetroot and pineapple topped with a burger. Pile the onion, egg, bacon and tomato sauce on top of the burger.

CHICKEN SANDWICH

SERVES 4

2 skinless chicken breast fillets, cut in half horizontally

2 tablespoons olive oil

2 tablespoons lemon juice

4 large pieces ciabatta or Turkish bread, cut in half horizontally

1 garlic clove, cut in half

mayonnaise

1 avocado, sliced

2 tomatoes, sliced

1 large handful of rocket (arugula) leaves, long stems snapped off

1 **Flatten out each piece** of chicken by hitting it either with your fist, the flat side of a knife blade or cleaver, or with a meat mallet. Don't break the flesh, just thin it out a bit. Trim off any fat or sinew.

2 **Cook the chicken** on a medium barbecue flatplate until brown and cooked through (you can check by cutting into the middle of one). Sprinkle with the lemon juice. Add the bread to the flatplate with the cut-side down and cook for a minute, pressing down on it to flatten it and help soak up any juices.

3 **Rub cut side of garlic** over the surface of the bread, then spread all the pieces with a generous amount of mayonnaise.

4 **Put a piece of chicken** on four of the pieces, season and then layer with the avocado and tomato, seasoning as you go. Finish with the rocket and the tops of the bread, then serve.

CHILLI BEEF BURGERS

SERVES 4

500 g (1 lb 2 oz) minced (ground) beef

6 red Asian shallots, finely chopped

25 g (1 oz/¼ cup) crisp fried onion flakes (see Note)

3 garlic cloves, finely chopped

2 long red chillies, seeded and finely chopped

20 g (¾ oz) finely chopped coriander (cilantro) leaves (include some stems)

2–2½ tablespoons chilli garlic sauce (see Note)

1 egg, lightly beaten

160 g (5¾ oz/2 cups) fresh breadcrumbs

olive oil, for brushing

1 loaf Turkish bread, cut into 4 pieces, or 4 round Turkish rolls

100 g (3½ oz) mignonette or green oak lettuce leaves

1   To make the burgers, put the beef, shallots, onion flakes, garlic, chilli, coriander, chilli garlic sauce, egg, breadcrumbs and 1½ teaspoons of salt in a large bowl, and knead well with your hands until the ingredients are thoroughly combined. Cover the bowl and refrigerate for 2 hours.

2   With wet hands, divide the beef mixture into four equal portions. Roll each portion into a ball, then flatten it slightly to form patties. Preheat the barbecue grill plate to medium direct heat. Brush patties lightly with oil. Cook for 5 minutes, then flip and cook for another 5–6 minutes, or until well browned and cooked through. A few minutes before the patties are done, toast the bread, cut-side down, on the grill for 1–2 minutes, or until marked and golden.

3   Divide the lettuce among four of the toasted bread slices. Add a patty, season the burgers with salt and pepper, then top with the remaining toasted bread.

Note: Crisp fried onion flakes and chilli garlic sauce are available from Asian grocery stores.

CHEESEBURGERS WITH CAPSICUM SALSA

SERVES 6

1 kg (2 lb 4 oz) minced (ground) beef

1 small onion, finely chopped

2 tablespoons chopped flat-leaf (Italian) parsley

1 teaspoon dried oregano

1 tablespoon tomato paste (purée)

70 g (2½ oz) cheddar cheese

6 bread rolls

salad leaves, to serve

CAPSICUM SALSA

2 red capsicums (peppers)

1 ripe tomato, finely chopped

1 small red onion, finely chopped

1 tablespoon olive oil

2 teaspoons red wine vinegar

1 **To make the salsa,** quarter the capsicums, remove the seeds and membranes and cook on a hot, lightly oiled barbecue grill, skin-side down, until the skin blackens and blisters. Place in a plastic bag and leave to cool. Peel away the skin and dice the flesh. Combine with the tomato, onion, olive oil and vinegar and leave for at least 1 hour to let the flavours develop. Serve at room temperature.

2 **Mix together the ground beef,** onion, herbs and tomato paste with your hands and season well. Divide into six portions and shape into six patties. Cut the cheese into small squares. Make a cavity in the top of each patty with your thumb. Place a piece of cheese in the cavity and smooth the mince over to enclose the cheese completely.

3 **Cook the patties on a hot,** lightly oiled barbecue grill or flatplate for 4–5 minutes each side, turning once. Serve in rolls with salad leaves and capsicum salsa.

Note: As a variation, try using camembert, brie or any blue cheese instead of the cheddar.

VEGETARIAN BURGERS WITH GARLIC CREAM

MAKES 10 BURGERS

250 g (9 oz/1 cup) red lentils

1 tablespoon oil

2 onions, sliced

1 tablespoon tandoori mix powder

425 g (15 oz) tin chickpeas, drained

1 tablespoon grated fresh ginger

1 egg

3 tablespoons chopped flat-leaf
(Italian) parsley

2 tablespoons chopped coriander
(cilantro) leaves

180 g (6½ oz/2¼ cups) fresh
breadcrumbs

plain (all-purpose) flour, for dusting

GARLIC CREAM

125 g (4½ oz/½ cup) sour cream

125 ml (4 fl oz/½ cup) cream

1 garlic clove, crushed

2 tablespoons chopped coriander
(cilantro) leaves

2 tablespoons chopped flat-leaf
(Italian) parsley

1   Simmer the lentils in a large pan of water for 8 minutes or until tender. Drain well. Heat the oil in a pan and cook the onion until tender. Add the tandoori mix and stir until fragrant.

2   Put the chickpeas, half the lentils, the ginger, egg and onion mixture in a food processor. Process for 20 seconds or until smooth. Transfer to a bowl. Stir in the remaining lentils, parsley, coriander and breadcrumbs.

3   Divide into 10 portions and shape into burgers (if the mixture is too soft, refrigerate for 15 minutes to firm). Toss the burgers in flour and place on a hot, lightly oiled barbecue grill or flatplate. Cook for 3–4 minutes each side or until browned.

4   For the coriander garlic cream, combine the sour cream, cream, garlic and herbs. Serve with the burgers.

ZUCCHINI PATTIES

MAKES 16

300 g (10½ oz) zucchini (courgette), grated

1 small onion, finely chopped

30 g (1 oz/¼ cup) self-raising flour

35 g (1¼ oz/⅓ cup) freshly grated kefalotyri or parmesan cheese

1 tablespoon chopped mint

2 teaspoons chopped flat-leaf (Italian) parsley

pinch freshly grated nutmeg

25 g (1 oz/¼ cup) dry breadcrumbs

1 egg, lightly beaten

olive oil, for pan-frying

lemon wedges, to serve

1 Put the zucchini and onion in the centre of a clean tea towel (dish towel), gather the corners together and twist as tightly as possible to remove all the juices. Combine the zucchini, onion, flour, cheese, mint, parsley, nutmeg, breadcrumbs and egg in a large bowl. Season well, then mix with your hands to form a stiff mixture that clumps together.

2 Preheat a barbecue flatplate to medium. When hot, drop level tablespoons of mixture onto the flatplate and cook for 2–3 minutes, or until well browned all over. Drain well on crumpled paper towels and serve hot, with lemon wedges.

PORK AND TOMATO BURGERS

SERVES 4

350 g (12 oz) minced (ground) pork and veal

100 g (3½ oz) sun-dried tomatoes, chopped

3 spring onions (scallions), finely chopped

2 tablespoons chopped basil

1 red capsicum (pepper), seeded and sliced

olive oil, for cooking

1 tablespoon balsamic vinegar

1 **Combine the pork and veal,** sun-dried tomato, spring onion and basil. Season well and knead for 2 minutes, or until a little sticky. Form into four burgers and refrigerate for at least 15 minutes.

2 **Mix the capsicum** with a little olive oil. Cook on a hot, lightly oiled barbecue grill or flatplate, tossing well and drizzling with balsamic vinegar, until just softened. Set aside.

3 **Wipe the barbecue** clean and reheat. Brush the burgers with a little olive oil and cook for 4–5 minutes each side, or until browned and cooked through. Serve with the capsicum.

HERBED LAMB BURGERS

MAKES 8 BURGERS

750 g (1 lb 10 oz) minced (ground) lamb

2 tablespoons chopped basil

1 tablespoon chopped chives

1 tablespoon chopped rosemary

1 tablespoon chopped thyme

2 tablespoons lemon juice

80 g (2¾ oz/1 cup) fresh breadcrumbs

1 egg

2 long crusty bread sticks

lettuce leaves, rinsed and dried

2 tomatoes, sliced

tomato sauce, to serve

1   Combine the lamb with the herbs, juice, breadcrumbs, egg and season well with salt and pepper. Mix well with your hands. Divide the mixture into eight portions and shape into thick rectangular patties.

2   Place the burgers on a hot, lightly oiled barbecue grill or flatplate. Cook for 5–10 minutes each side until well browned and just cooked through.

3   Cut the bread sticks in half and sandwich with the burgers, lettuce, tomato and tomato sauce.

PORK SAUSAGE BURGERS WITH MUSTARD CREAM

SERVES 6

800 g (1 lb 12 oz) minced (ground) pork

1 small onion, finely chopped

80 g (2¾ oz/1 cup) fresh breadcrumbs

2 garlic cloves, crushed

1 egg, lightly beaten

1 teaspoon dried sage

6 long bread rolls

MUSTARD CREAM

125 g (4½ oz/½ cup) sour cream

1 tablespoon wholegrain mustard

2 teaspoons lemon juice

1 **Combine the pork,** onion, breadcrumbs, garlic, egg and sage with your hands. Season well. Divide the mixture into six portions and shape into sausages.

2 **Cook the sausages** on a hot, lightly oiled barbecue flatplate or grill for 5–10 minutes, turning occasionally.

3 **To make the mustard cream,** put the sour cream, mustard and juice in a small bowl and stir together. Spread each cut side of the rolls with a little mustard cream, then sandwich the sausage burgers in the middle. Serve with the remaining mustard cream.

YAKITORI CHICKEN BURGERS

SERVES 4

4 chicken thigh fillets, trimmed

185 ml (6 fl oz/¾ cup) yakitori sauce

1 teaspoon cornflour (cornstarch)

oil, for brushing

4 soft hamburger buns, halved

80 g (2¾ oz/⅓ cup) Japanese mayonnaise (see Note)

80 g (2¾ oz) mizuna lettuce

1 Lebanese (short) cucumber, ends trimmed and shaved into ribbons with a vegetable peeler

1 Toss the chicken and yakitori sauce together in a bowl until the chicken fillets are well coated, then cover and refrigerate for 4 hours.

2 Drain the yakitori sauce from the chicken into a small saucepan and sprinkle it with the cornflour. Stir the cornflour into the marinade, bring the mixture to the boil and simmer, stirring frequently, for 5 minutes, or until it is thickened, then keep it warm.

3 Lightly brush the barbecue grill with oil and preheat it to low–medium direct heat. Cook the chicken on the grill for about 6 minutes on each side, or until cooked through. Toast the burger buns for about 1 minute on each side, or until they are marked and golden.

4 Spread some mayonnaise on the inside surface of each bun, cover the base with mizuna and cucumber ribbons, and top with the chicken. Spread some of the thickened marinade over the chicken and top with the other half of the bun.

Note: Japanese mayonnaise is available in larger supermarkets and Asian speciality stores. If you can't find it, use good-quality regular whole-egg mayonnaise instead.

HAMBURGERS WITH FRESH CORN RELISH

SERVES 4

700 g (1 lb 9 oz) minced (ground) beef

1 garlic clove

1½ onions, very finely chopped

2 tablespoons parsley, finely chopped

1 tablespoon tomato ketchup

¼ teaspoon worcestershire sauce

2 corn cobs

2 tomatoes, finely chopped

1 tablespoon sweet chilli sauce

1 handful coriander (cilantro) leaves

lime juice

1 tablespoon oil

4 bread buns

baby cos (romaine) leaves

1 **Turn on the grill (broiler).** Put the beef in a bowl with the garlic, half of the onion, the parsley, tomato ketchup and the Worcestershire sauce. Season and mix well, then leave it to marinate while you make the relish.

2 **Grill the corn cob** on all sides until it is slightly blackened and charred around the edges. By this time it should be cooked through. Slice off the kernels by slicing down the length of the cob with a sharp knife. Mix the kernels with the tomato, chilli sauce, coriander and remaining onion.

3 **Add lime juice** and salt and pepper, to taste.

4 **Form the beef mixture** into four large patties and flatten them out to the size of the buns (bear in mind that they will shrink as they cook).

5 **Preheat a barbecue** flatplate to medium–high. Cook the the beef patties for 3–5 minutes on each side, depending on how well cooked you like them. While they are cooking, toast the buns.

6 **Lay a lettuce leaf** or two on each bun bottom, add some relish and top with a hamburger patty and the bun top. Serve any extra relish on the side.

LAMB BURGERS

SERVES 4

1 tablespoon ground cumin

250 g (9 oz/1 cup) plain Greek-style yoghurt

½ Lebanese (short) cucumber, grated

1 tablespoon finely chopped mint leaves

1 tablespoon olive oil

1 onion, finely chopped

2 garlic cloves, crushed

800 g (1 lb 12 oz) minced (ground) lamb

2 tablespoons finely chopped flat-leaf (Italian) parsley

2 tablespoons finely chopped coriander (cilantro) leaves

2 red capsicums (peppers), quartered and seeded

1 tablespoon olive oil, extra

2 red onions, thinly sliced

olive oil spray

1 loaf Turkish bread, cut into 4 pieces and split horizontally

100 g (3½ oz) baby rocket (arugula) leaves

1 **Dry-fry 1 teaspoon** ground cumin over medium heat for 30 seconds, or until it is fragrant. Put the yoghurt, cucumber, mint and dry-fried cumin in a small bowl and combine well. Cover the bowl and refrigerate it until needed.

2 **Heat the oil** in a frying pan and cook the onion over medium heat for 2–3 minutes or until softened. Add the garlic and remaining cumin, cook it for another minute, then allow the mixture to cool. Put the onion mixture in a large bowl with the lamb, parsley and coriander, season with salt and pepper and mix it together with your hands. Divide the mixture into four even portions, and shape each one into a 2 cm (¾ inch) thick patty.

3 **Heat the barbecue** flatplate to medium–high direct heat. Toss the capsicum with the extra oil and cook on the flatplate for 6 minutes on each side or until it is softened and lightly charred. Cook the patties on the flatplate for 5–6 minutes each side or until they are done.

4 **Spray the red onion** with the olive oil spray and cook it on the flatplate for 2–3 minutes or until soft and golden. Toast the bread, cut-side down, on the grill for 1–2 minutes or until it is marked and golden.

5 **To assemble the burgers,** put some rocket on four of the bread slices. Put a patty on top, then the capsicum and onion. Dollop 2–3 tablespoons of the yoghurt mixture on each and season with salt and freshly ground black pepper. Top with the remaining bread slices and serve them straight away.

CHICKPEA BURGERS

MAKES 6

1 eggplant (aubergine), cut into 1 cm (½ inch) slices

olive oil, for brushing

1 large red onion, sliced into rings

2 large handfuls rocket (arugula) leaves

6 pieces Turkish bread

CHICKPEA PATTIES

2 teaspoons olive oil

1 small onion, finely chopped

2 garlic cloves, crushed

2 x 400 g (14 oz) tin chickpeas, rinsed and drained

95 g (3½ oz/½ cup) cooked brown rice

50 g (1¾ oz/⅓ cup) sun-dried tomatoes, chopped

SPICY YOGHURT DRESSING

200 g (7 oz) thick plain yoghurt

1 garlic clove, crushed

¼ teaspoon ground cumin

¼ teaspoon ground coriander

1 **To make the chickpea patties,** heat the oil in a frying pan and cook the onion over medium heat for 2 minutes, or until soft and lightly golden. Add the garlic and cook for 1 more minute, then remove from the heat and allow to cool slightly. Put the onion mixture in a food processor with the chickpeas, rice and sun-dried tomato. Using a pulse action, process in short bursts until the mixture is combined and the chickpeas are broken up, but not completely mushy, scraping the bowl down with a spatula a few times during processing. Season to taste, then shape the mixture into six patties about 8 cm (3¼ in) in diameter. Place on a tray lined with plastic wrap, then cover and refrigerate for 1 hour.

2 **Put all the spicy yoghurt dressing** ingredients in a small bowl and mix together well. Refrigerate until needed.

3 **Preheat a barbecue** flatplate to hot. Brush the eggplant slices lightly on each side with oil, and toss a little oil through the onion rings. Cook the eggplant and onion on the flatplate until tender and lightly golden — the eggplant will need about 3–4 minutes each side, the onion about 5 minutes. Transfer the vegetables to a plate and set aside.

4 **Brush the top** of the chickpea patties lightly with oil, then put them face-down on the flatplate and cook for 3 minutes. Brush the top of the patties with a little oil, then turn and cook for a further 3 minutes, or until golden. They may stick a little, so get the spatula well underneath before turning.

5 **While the chickpea patties are cooking,** arrange the rocket, barbecued eggplant and onion on the Turkish bread slices. Add the hot chickpea patties, dollop with some of the spicy yoghurt dressing and serve at once.

SARDINE PATTIES

MAKES 6

450 g (1 lb) sardines, gutted

1 thick slice of white bread, crusts removed

1 large garlic clove, crushed

2 tablespoons chopped parsley

pinch of ground cumin

pinch of ground paprika

2 large eggs, lightly beaten

40 g (1½ oz/⅓ cup) plain (all-purpose) flour, plus a little extra, for dusting

3–4 tablespoons oil

lemon wedges, to serve

1 Cut each sardine into two fillets and remove the flesh from the skins. Remove as many of the bones as possible using tweezers. Roughly chop the flesh and put in a bowl.

2 Put the bread in a food processor and whiz to make fine breadcrumbs or chop finely by hand. Add the fish, garlic, parsley, cumin, paprika, beaten egg and flour and process until roughly combined. Season with salt. With lightly floured hands, form the mixture into six even balls. Put on a plate, cover and chill in the fridge for 30 minutes before cooking.

3 Preheat a barbecue flatplate to medium–high. Add three balls of mixture and flatten them out slightly to a patty shape. Cook for 4–5 minutes on each side, or until golden brown and cooked through. Drain them on crumpled paper towels and keep warm. Repeat with the rest of the balls, adding more oil, if necessary. Serve with the lemon wedges.

STEAK SANDWICH WITH SALSA VERDE

SERVES 4

2 garlic cloves, crushed

4 handfuls parsley

½ bunch basil leaves

½ bunch mint leaves

3 tablespoons olive oil

2 teaspoons capers, chopped

2 teaspoons lemon juice

2 teaspoons red wine vinegar

4 minute steaks

4 large pieces ciabatta or Turkish bread, halved horizontally

1 Lebanese (short) cucumber, sliced

1 **To make the salsa verde,** put the garlic and herbs in a food processor with 2 tablespoons of the oil and whizz them together until they are coarsely chopped. Tip chopped herbs into a bowl and stir in the capers, lemon juice and vinegar. Season with salt and pepper.

2 **Preheat a barbecue flatplate** to medium–high. Cook the steaks for 1 minute on each side — they should cook very quickly and start to brown.

3 **While the steaks are cooking,** toast the bread. Spread some salsa verde on all the pieces of the bread and make four sandwiches with the steaks and cucumber.

LAMB SOUVLAKI ROLL

SERVES 4

500 g (1 lb 2 oz) lamb backstrap or loin fillet

100 ml (3½ fl oz) olive oil

3 tablespoons dry white wine

1 tablespoon chopped oregano

3 tablespoons roughly chopped basil

3 garlic cloves, crushed

2 bay leaves, crushed

2½ tablespoons lemon juice

1 large loaf Turkish bread

250 g (9 oz/1 cup) baba ghanoush

1 tablespoon roughly chopped flat-leaf (Italian) parsley

1 **Place the lamb fillet** in a shallow non-metallic dish. Combine the oil, wine, oregano, basil, garlic, bay leaves and 2 tablespoons of the lemon juice and pour over the lamb, turning to coat well. Cover with plastic wrap and marinate for 4 hours in a cool place.

2 **Remove the lamb fillet** from the marinade and cook on a hot, lightly oiled barbecue grill or flatplate for 6–8 minutes, or until seared but still pink in the centre. Remove from the heat and rest for 10 minutes, then cut into slices.

3 **Split Turkish bread** lengthways and spread the bottom thickly with baba ghanoush. Top with lamb slices, sprinkle with parsley and remaining lemon juice, then season with salt and pepper. Replace the top of the loaf. Cut into quarters to serve.

STEAK BAGUETTE WITH ROCKET AND MUSTARDY MAYO

SERVES 4

3 tablespoons olive oil, plus extra
  for frying

1 red onion, sliced

1 teaspoon brown sugar

2 teaspoons balsamic vinegar

1 teaspoon thyme

1 tablespoon Dijon mustard

3 tablespoons mayonnaise

100 g (3½ oz) rocket (arugula)

500 g (1 lb 2 oz) beef fillet, cut into
  4 thin slices

2 thick baguettes, cut in half, or 8 thick
  slices of good-quality bread

2 tomatoes, sliced

1   Heat 2 tablespoons oil in a small saucepan. Add the onion and cook very slowly, with the lid on, stirring occasionally, until the onion is soft but not brown. This could take up to 15 minutes. Remove the lid, add the sugar and vinegar and cook for a further 10 minutes, or until the onion is soft and just browned. Take the pan off the stove and stir in the thyme.

2   Meanwhile, make the mustardy mayo by mixing together well the mustard and mayonnaise in a small bowl.

3   Drizzle the rocket leaves with the remaining olive oil and season with salt and freshly ground black pepper.

4   Preheat a barbecue flatplate to medium–high. Cook the steaks for 2 minutes on each side, adding more oil if necessary. Season to taste.

5   To serve, put out the bread, along with separate bowls containing the onion, mustardy mayo, rocket leaves, steak and sliced tomatoes. Let everyone make their own baguette so they can get the perfect mix of all the flavours.

JUMBO SPICY LAMB BURGERS

SERVES 4

2 red capsicums (peppers)

1 eggplant (aubergine), cut into 8 thick slices

3 tablespoons olive oil

3 teaspoons ground cumin

2 teaspoons ground coriander

1 teaspoon ground cardamom

½ teaspoon ground cinnamon

3 tablespoons chopped coriander (cilantro) stems and leaves

750 g (1 lb 10 oz) minced (ground) lamb

1 small red onion, diced

oil, for brushing

8 thick slices sourdough bread

200 g (7 oz) baba ghanoush

60 g (2 oz) baby rocket (arugula) leaves

125 g (4½ oz/½ cup) whole-egg mayonnaise

3 garlic cloves, crushed

1 **Heat the grill (broiler) to high.** Cut the capsicums into quarters, discarding the seeds and membrane. Arrange skin-side-up on the grill tray and grill until the skin blackens and blisters. Leave to cool in a plastic bag, then peel away the skin.

2 **Meanwhile, preheat a barbecue flatplate** or grill to high. Toss the eggplant in the oil to coat and cook for 2–3 minutes on each side, or until golden and softened. Remove from the heat. Turn the barbecue down to moderately high.

3 **Dry-fry the ground cumin,** coriander, cardamom and cinnamon in a frying pan over medium heat for 1 minute or until fragrant, taking care not to let the spices burn. Put the fried spices in a bowl with the chopped coriander, lamb and onion and season. Mix until well combined, then form into four burgers about 1 cm (½ inch) thick.

4 **Brush the hotplate** with oil and cook the lamb burgers for 4–5 minutes on each side, or until cooked through.

5 **Meanwhile, grill the bread** until toasted on both sides. Spread the baba ghanoush over 4 of the slices and top with the rocket, eggplant, capsicum and lamb burgers. Mix the mayonnaise and garlic together and dollop over the burgers. Top with the remaining bread halves and serve immediately.

SALMON AND DILL POTATO PATTIES WITH LIME MAYO

SERVES 4

400 g (14 oz) new potatoes, cut in half

2 teaspoons grated lime rind

310 g (11 oz/1¼ cups) whole-egg mayonnaise

425 g (15 oz) tin salmon, drained, bones removed

1 tablespoon chopped fresh dill

2 spring onions (scallions), thinly sliced

1 egg

80 g (2¾ oz/1 cup) fresh breadcrumbs

60 ml (2 fl oz/¼ cup) oil

200 g (7 oz) rocket leaves

lime wedges, to serve

1   Cook the potatoes in a large saucepan of boiling water for 12–15 minutes, or until tender. Drain well and cool.

2   Meanwhile, combine lime rind and 250 g (9 oz/1 cup) of the mayonnaise.

3   Transfer the potato to a large bowl, then mash roughly with the back of a spoon, leaving some large chunks. Stir in the salmon, dill and spring onion and season. Mix in the egg and the remaining mayonnaise. Divide into eight portions, forming palm-size patties. Press lightly into the breadcrumbs to coat.

4   Preheat a barbecue flatplate to medium. Cook the patties, turning, for 3–4 minutes, or until golden brown. Drain on paper towels. Serve with a dollop of lime mayonnaise, rocket leaves and lime wedges.

FISH BURGERS AND WEDGES

SERVES 4

500 g (1 lb 2 oz) skinless flake fillets

2 tablespoons finely chopped parsley

2 tablespoons finely chopped dill

2 tablespoons lemon juice

1 tablespoon capers, drained, rinsed and chopped

2 gherkins, finely chopped

350 g (12 oz) potatoes, cooked and mashed

plain (all-purpose) flour, for dusting

1 tablespoon olive oil

4 hamburger buns, split into halves

lettuce leaves

2 roma (plum) tomatoes, sliced

tartare sauce, for serving

CRUNCHY POTATO WEDGES

6 potatoes

1 tablespoon oil, plus extra, for deep-frying

½ teaspoon chicken salt

25 g (1 oz/¼ cup) dry breadcrumbs

2 teaspoons chopped chives

1 teaspoon celery salt

¼ teaspoon garlic powder

½ teaspoon chopped rosemary

1 **Put the fish fillets** in a frying pan and add enough water so that the fish is just covered. Slowly heat the water, making sure it doesn't come to the boil. Cover with a lid and cook over low heat until the fish is just cooked through. Drain the fish on crumpled paper towels, then transfer to a bowl and flake the flesh with a fork, removing any bones.

2 **Add the parsley,** dill, lemon juice, capers, gherkins and potato to the bowl with the fish, then season with freshly ground black pepper and some salt, and mix well. Divide the mixture into four and shape each portion into a patty. Lightly dust the patties with flour, cover and refrigerate for 1 hour—this will help them stick together during cooking.

3 **While the patties are resting,** make the wedges. Preheat the oven to 200°C (400°F/Gas 6). Wash the potatoes, then cut them into wedges, leaving the skin on. Pat the potato wedges dry with paper towels and then toss with the oil so they are all covered. Combine the chicken salt, breadcrumbs, chives, celery salt, garlic powder and rosemary, and then toss with the wedges. Spread the wedges out onto greased baking trays and bake for 40 minutes, or until golden.

4 **Preheat a barbecue flatplate** to medium. Cook the fish patties for 5–6 minutes on each side, or until well browned and cooked through.

5 **Grill the buns** and butter them if you wish. On each base, put some lettuce, tomato, a fish patty and some tartare sauce. Top with the other half of the bun and serve with the hot potato wedges.

LAMB AND HUMMUS WRAPS

SERVES 4

500 g (1 lb 2 oz) minced (ground) lamb

1 onion, finely chopped

2–3 garlic cloves, chopped

1 tablespoon za'atar (Middle Eastern spice mix), plus extra, for sprinkling

30 g (1 oz) coriander (cilantro) leaves

olive oil

4 Lebanese (large pitta) breads, to serve

75 g (2½ oz) mixed salad leaves

HUMMUS

300 g (10½ oz) tinned chickpeas

2 garlic cloves, crushed

1 tablespoon tahini paste

3 tablespoons lemon juice

1 Put the lamb, onion, garlic, za'atar and coriander leaves in a food processor and blend until smooth and pasty. Put into a bowl, cover and refrigerate for 1 hour.

2 With wet hands, form meat into eight 12 cm (4½ inch) elongated sausage shapes. Heat a barbecue flatplate or grill and coat with oil. Coat the lamb with the oil. Cook and turn for 8 minutes, or until evenly browned and cooked through.

3 Meanwhile, to make the hummus, drain the chickpeas, reserving the liquid and put in a food processor or blender. Add the garlic and tahini. With the motor running, add the lemon juice and 3 tablespoons of reserved chickpea liquid. Process until smooth. Add a little more lemon juice and reserved liquid, if desired, and season with salt and freshly ground black pepper.

4 Lightly brush one side of the Lebanese breads with oil and sprinkle with the za'atar. Put the unoiled side on the chargrill or hotplate for 2–3 minutes, or until heated through.

5 To serve, place the Lebanese breads on serving plates. Generously spread over the hummus. Top each with two of the lamb sausages and some salad leaves and roll up firmly.

MEDITERRANEAN BURGERS

SERVES 4

1 large red capsicum (pepper)

500 g (1 lb 2 oz) minced (ground) lamb

1 egg, lightly beaten

1 small onion, grated

3 garlic cloves, crushed

2 tablespoons pine nuts, chopped

1 tablespoon finely chopped mint

1 tablespoon finely chopped flat-leaf (Italian) parsley

1 teaspoon ground cumin

2 teaspoons chilli sauce

1 tablespoon olive oil

4 Turkish or pide bread rolls

220 g (7¾ oz/1 cup) ready-made hummus

100 g (3½ oz) baby rocket

1 small Lebanese (short) cucumber, cut into ribbons

chilli sauce, to serve (optional)

1   Cut the capsicum into large pieces, removing the seeds and membrane. Place, skin-side-up, under a hot grill (broiler) until the skin blackens and blisters. Cool in a plastic bag, then peel and cut into thick strips.

2   Combine the lamb, egg, onion, garlic, pine nuts, fresh herbs, cumin and chilli sauce in a large bowl. Mix with your hands and roll into four even-sized balls. Press the balls into large patties about 9 cm (3½ inches) in diameter.

3   Preheat a barbecue flatplate to medium. Cook the patties for 6 minutes each side, or until well browned and cooked through, then drain on paper towels.

4   Halve the rolls and toast both sides. Spread the cut sides of the rolls with hummus, then lay rocket leaves, roasted capsicum and cucumber ribbons over the base. Place a patty on the salad and top with the other half of the roll. Serve with chilli sauce.

MAINS

CHICKEN DRUMSTICKS WITH RANCH DRESSING

MAKES 32

32 small chicken drumsticks

1 tablespoon garlic salt

1 tablespoon onion powder

oil, for deep-frying

250 ml (9 fl oz/1 cup) tomato sauce (ketchup)

80 ml (2½ fl oz/⅓ cup) worcestershire sauce

40 g (1½ oz) butter, melted

1 tablespoon sugar

Tabasco sauce, to taste

RANCH DRESSING

250 g (9 oz/1 cup) whole-egg mayonnaise

250 g (9 oz/1 cup) sour cream

80 ml (2½ fl oz/⅓ cup) lemon juice

20 g (¾ oz/⅓ cup) snipped chives

1   Remove the skin from the chicken and use a cleaver or large knife to cut off the knuckle. Wash the chicken thoroughly and pat dry with paper towels. Combine 1 tablespoon cracked black pepper, and the garlic salt and onion powder and rub some into each piece of chicken.

2   Fill a deep heavy-based frying pan one-third full of oil and heat the oil to 180°C (350°F), or when a cube of bread dropped into the oil turns golden brown in 15 seconds. Cook the chicken in batches for 2 minutes each batch, remove with tongs or a slotted spoon and drain on paper towels.

3   Transfer chicken to a large non-metallic bowl or shallow dish. Combine sauces, butter, sugar and Tabasco. Pour over the chicken, stirring to coat. Refrigerate, covered, for several hours or overnight. Prepare and heat the barbecue 1 hour before cooking.

4   Put the chicken on a lightly oiled hot barbecue grill or flatplate and cook for 20–25 minutes, or until cooked through. Turn and brush with the marinade during cooking. Serve with the ranch dressing.

5   To make the ranch dressing, combine the mayonnaise, sour cream, juice, chives, and season to taste.

BARBECUED HONEY CHICKEN WINGS

SERVES 4

12 chicken wings

4 tablespoons soy sauce

3 tablespoons sherry

3 tablespoons oil

1 garlic clove, crushed

3 tablespoons honey

1   **Rinse the chicken wings,** then give them a thorough pat with paper towels to dry them. Tuck the wing tips into the underside.

2   **Put the chicken wings** in a shallow non-metallic dish. Whisk together the soy sauce, sherry, oil and garlic, then pour all over the chicken wings, lightly tossing for good measure. Cover with plastic wrap, then leave in the fridge for 2 hours to give the chicken a chance to take up some of the marinade — it will help if you turn the wings occasionally.

3   **The honey needs** to be heated enough for it to become brushing consistency — either use the microwave or warm it gently in a small saucepan.

4   **Lightly grease a barbecue** flatplate or grill and heat to medium. Cook the chicken wings until tender and cooked through, turning occasionally — this should take about 12 minutes. Brush the wings with the warmed honey and cook for 2 minutes more.

PEPPER STEAKS WITH HORSERADISH SAUCE

SERVES 4

4 sirloin steaks

3 tablespoons seasoned cracked pepper

HORSERADISH SAUCE

2 tablespoons brandy

3 tablespoons beef stock

4 tablespoons cream

1 tablespoon horseradish cream

½ teaspoon sugar

1 **Coat the steaks** on both sides with pepper, pressing it into the meat. Cook on a hot, lightly oiled barbecue grill or flatplate for 5–10 minutes, or until cooked to your taste.

2 **To make the sauce,** put the brandy and stock in a pan. Bring to the boil, then reduce the heat. Stir in the cream, horseradish and sugar and heat through. Serve with the steaks.

PORK LOIN WITH APPLE GLAZE AND WEDGES

SERVES 6–8

1 teaspoon aniseed

135 g (4¾ oz/½ cup) apple sauce

2 tablespoons soft brown sugar

1.5 kg (3 lb 5 oz) boned pork loin with the skin on

2 teaspoons oil

1 tablespoon salt

4 large potatoes, each cut into 8 wedges

2 tablespoons olive oil

2 teaspoons garlic salt

1 **Dry-fry the aniseed** over medium heat for 30 seconds, or until it becomes fragrant. Add the apple sauce and brown sugar, reduce the heat to low and cook, stirring, for 1 minute.

2 **Use a sharp knife** to remove the skin from the pork loin. Score the skin in a diamond pattern and rub the oil and salt over the skin, working into the cuts. Put the potato wedges in a bowl with the olive oil and garlic salt, season with black pepper and toss until well coated.

3 **Preheat a kettle** or covered barbecue to medium indirect heat. Tie the pork loin with string to help keep its shape, then put the pork and the skin in the barbecue and arrange the wedges around them. After 30 minutes, baste the pork with the apple glaze, and repeat every 10 minutes for a further 30 minutes (for 1 hour cooking time in all). Turn the skin and the wedges as you go so that they cook evenly.

4 **When pork is ready,** remove it from the barbecue and leave to rest, covered, for 10 minutes before carving. Cut the crackling with a sharp knife, arrange it on a serving platter with the pork and serve with the potato wedges. This is delicious served with coleslaw.

VEAL STEAKS WITH CAPER BUTTER

SERVES 4

50 g (1¾ oz) butter, softened

2 tablespoons dry white wine

2 tablespoons capers, finely chopped

2 teaspoons finely grated lemon zest

8 small veal steaks, about 500 g
   (1 lb 2 oz)

mixed salad greens, to serve

1 **Combine the butter,** white wine, capers, lemon zest and some salt and black pepper with a wooden spoon. Shape into a log, cover and refrigerate until required.

2 **Cook the veal steaks** on a hot, lightly oiled barbecue flatplate or grill for 2–3 minutes on each side. Remove, place on warm plates and top with slices of the caper butter. Serve immediately on a bed of salad greens.

BEEF WITH BLUE CHEESE BUTTER

SERVES 4

100 g (3½ oz) butter, softened

2 garlic cloves, crushed

100 g (3½ oz) Blue Castello cheese

2 teaspoons finely shredded sage leaves

1 kg (2 lb 4 oz) beef eye fillet (thick end), trimmed

1 tablespoon olive oil

1 To make the blue cheese butter, mash together the softened butter, garlic, cheese and sage until they are well combined. Form the mixture into a log and wrap it in baking paper, twisting the ends to seal them. Refrigerate the butter until firm, then cut it into 5 mm (¼ inch) slices and leave it at room temperature until needed.

2 Cut the beef into four thick, equal pieces and tie a piece of string around the edge of each so it will keep its shape during cooking. Brush both sides of each steak with the oil and season with freshly ground pepper. Heat a barbecue to medium–high direct heat and cook the beef on the grill for 6–7 minutes each side for medium, or to your liking.

3 Put two slices of blue cheese butter on top of each steak as soon as you remove it from the barbecue. Remove string.

Note: Any leftover butter can be wrapped in baking paper and foil, and frozen for up to 2 months. It is also delicious served with chicken and pork.

GREEK PEPPER LAMB SALAD

SERVES 4

300 g (10½ oz) lamb backstraps

1½ tablespoons cracked black pepper

3 vine-ripened tomatoes, cut into 8 wedges

2 Lebanese (short) cucumbers, sliced

150 g (5½ oz) lemon and garlic marinated Kalamata olives, drained (reserving 1½ tablespoons oil)

100 g (3½ oz) feta cheese, cubed

¾ teaspoon dried oregano

1 tablespoon lemon juice

1 tablespoon extra virgin olive oil

1   Roll the backstraps in the pepper, pressing the pepper on with your fingers. Cover and refrigerate for about 15 minutes. Place the tomato, cucumber, olives, feta and ½ teaspoon of the dried oregano in a bowl.

2   Heat a barbecue flatplate, brush with oil and when very hot, cook the lamb for 2–3 minutes on each side, or until cooked to your liking. Keep warm.

3   Whisk the lemon juice, extra virgin olive oil, reserved Kalamata oil and the remaining dried oregano together well. Season. Pour half the dressing over the salad, toss together and arrange on a serving platter.

4   Cut the lamb on the diagonal into 1 cm (½ inch) thick slices and arrange on top of the salad. Pour the rest of the dressing on top and serve.

CHARGRILLED ASPARAGUS AND CHICKEN

SERVES 4

6 (about 225 g /8 oz) chicken tenderloins

16 asparagus spears, trimmed

1 handful small mint leaves

½, seeded and finely shredded long green chilli

DRESSING

80 ml (2½ fl oz/⅓ cup) oil

2 tablespoons coconut milk

2 teaspoons lime juice

1 teaspoon grated makrut (kaffir lime) zest

2 garlic cloves, crushed

½ teaspoon finely chopped mint

1 **To make the dressing,** put half the oil, the coconut milk, lime juice, lime zest and garlic in a small bowl and season with a little salt and plenty of freshly ground black pepper. Mix well.

2 **Trim the white sinew** from the thick end of the chicken tenderloins and halve them lengthways. Put the chicken and asparagus spears in a shallow non-metallic dish. Pour in half the dressing and toss to coat. Set aside to marinate for 30 minutes. Add the remaining oil and the mint to the other half of the dressing.

3 **Spray a hot barbecue flatplate** with oil. Remove the asparagus and chicken from the marinade, drain and cook for 7–8 minutes, or until browned and cooked through, turning the asparagus often and the chicken once. Discard the marinade.

4 **Transfer the asparagus** and chicken to a bowl, add the mint leaves and chilli and toss lightly. Pile in the centre of 4 plates and drizzle with the dressing. Serve warm or at room temperature.

SWORDFISH WITH TOMATO BUTTER AND ASPARAGUS

SERVES 4

100 g (3½ oz) butter, softened

50 g (1¾ oz/⅓ cup) semi-dried (sun-blushed) tomatoes, finely chopped

2 tablespoons baby capers in brine, drained and crushed

1½ tablespoons shredded basil leaves

4 garlic cloves, crushed

3 tablespoons extra virgin olive oil

300 g (10½ oz) slender asparagus spears, trimmed

4 swordfish steaks

1   Put the butter in a bowl with the tomato, capers, basil and two cloves of crushed garlic, and mash it all together. Shape the flavoured butter into a log, then wrap it in baking paper and twist the ends to close them off. Refrigerate until the butter is firm, then cut it into 1 cm (½ in) slices and leave it, covered, at room temperature until needed.

2   Mix 2 tablespoons of the oil and the remaining garlic in a small bowl. Toss the asparagus spears with the oil until they are well coated, season them with salt and pepper, and leave for 30 minutes.

3   Preheat a ridged barbecue grill to high direct heat. Brush the swordfish steaks with the remaining oil and cook them for 2–3 minutes on each side or until they are just cooked through. Don't overcook the fish as residual heat will continue to cook the meat after it has been removed from the barbecue. Put a piece of the tomato butter on top of each steak as soon as it comes off the barbecue and season to taste. Cook the asparagus on the gril, turning it regularly, for 2–3 minutes, or until it is just tender. Serve the asparagus immediately with the fish.

GRILLED RED MULLET WITH HERB SAUCE

SERVES 4

4 x 200 g (7 oz) red mullet
60 ml (2 fl oz/¼ cup) lemon juice
60 ml (2 fl oz/¼ cup) olive oil
parsley, for garnish
lemon wedges, to serve

HERB SAUCE

100 g (3½ oz) English or baby spinach
60 ml (2 fl oz/¼ cup) olive oil
1 tablespoon white wine vinegar
1 tablespoon chopped parsley
1 tablespoon chopped chives
1 tablespoon chopped chervil
1 tablespoon finely chopped capers
2 anchovy fillets, finely chopped
1 hard-boiled egg, finely chopped

1   Preheat the barbecue flatplate or grill. Make a couple of deep slashes in the thickest part of each fish. Pat the fish dry and sprinkle inside and out with salt and pepper. Drizzle with a little lemon juice and olive oil and cook on the barbecue for 4–5 minutes each side, or until the fish flakes when tested with a knife tip. Baste with lemon juice and oil during cooking.

2   To make the sauce, wash the spinach and place in a large saucepan with just the water clinging to the leaves. Cover pan and steam the spinach for 2 minutes, or until just wilted. Drain, cool and squeeze with your hands to get rid of excess liquid. Finely chop. Mix with the oil, vinegar, herbs, capers, anchovy and egg in a food processor or mortar and pestle. Spoon the sauce onto a plate and place the fish on top to serve.

SPICED GRILLED CHICKEN

SERVES 4

2 x 750 g (1 lb 10 oz) chickens

pinch of saffron threads

1 teaspoon coarse salt

2 garlic cloves, chopped

1½ teaspoons paprika

¼ teaspoon cayenne pepper

2 teaspoons ground cumin

½ teaspoon freshly ground black pepper

1 tablespoon lemon juice

1 tablespoon olive oil

2 lemons

2 tablespoons icing (confectioners') sugar

watercress, picked over, to garnish

1 To prepare the chickens, cut them on each side of the backbone using poultry shears or kitchen scissors. Rinse the chickens and dry with paper towels. Open out on a board, skin side up, and press down with the heel of your hand on the top of each breast to break the breastbone and flatten it. Cut deep slashes diagonally in each breast and across the legs. Using two long metal skewers for each chicken, push the skewers from the tip of each breast through to the underside of the legs, which should be spread outwards so that the thickness of the chicken is as even as possible.

2 Put the saffron in a mortar with the salt and pound with a pestle to pulverise the threads. Add the garlic and pound to a paste. Work in the paprika, cayenne pepper, cumin, black pepper, lemon juice and olive oil. Rub the spice mix into the chickens, rubbing it into the slashes. Cover and marinate in

the refrigerator for at least 2 hours, or overnight. Bring the chickens to room temperature 1 hour before cooking.

3 Preheat the barbecue and place chickens on the grill, skin side up. Cook over medium heat for 20 minutes, continually turning the chicken as it cooks and brushing with remaining marinade. The chicken is cooked if the juices run clear when the thigh is pierced. Transfer chickens to a platter, remove the skewers, cover with a foil tent and leave to rest for 5 minutes before cutting in half to serve.

4 Quarter the lemons and dip the cut surfaces in the sifted icing sugar. Place on the barbecue flatplate. Cook on the cut surfaces until golden and caramelised. Serve the chickens with the lemon quarters and watercress.

BACON-WRAPPED CHICKEN

SERVES 6

2 tablespoons olive oil

2 tablespoons lime juice

¼ teaspoon ground coriander

6 chicken breast fillets

4 tablespoons fruit chutney

3 tablespoons chopped pecan nuts

6 bacon slices

1 **Combine the olive oil,** lime juice, coriander and salt and pepper. Using a sharp knife, cut a pocket in the thickest section of each chicken fillet. Combine chutney and nuts and spoon 1 tablespoon of the mixture into each pocket.

2 **Turn the tapered ends** of the fillets to the underside. Wrap a slice of bacon around each fillet to enclose the filling; secure with a toothpick.

3 **Put the chicken parcels** on a hot, lightly oiled barbecue grill or flatplate and cook for 5 minutes on each side, or until cooked through, turning once. Brush with lime juice mixture several times during cooking and drizzle with leftover juice mixture when serving.

BLACKENED SNAPPER

SERVES 6

6 large skinless snapper fillets, 2 cm
(¾ inch) thick

125 g (4½ oz) unsalted butter, melted

2 tablespoons Cajun spice mix

2 teaspoons sweet paprika

lemon wedges, to serve

1 **Brush each fish fillet** liberally with the melted butter.

2 **Combine the Cajun spice mix** and paprika, then sprinkle thickly over the fish. Use your fingers to rub the spice mix evenly over the fillets.

3 **Preheat a barbecue flatplate** to high. Cook two fillets at a time in the pan for 1–2 minutes on one side. Turn and cook for another few minutes, or until the fish is cooked and flakes easily. The surface should be well charred on each side. Add extra butter if necessary. Serve drizzled with any remaining melted butter and lemon wedges—they can be served lightly charred if you like.

FISH WITH WATERCRESS AND GREEN PEA SAUCE

SERVES 4

4 mahi-mahi fillets (or other firm white fish fillets)

plain (all-purpose) flour, for dusting

250 g (9 oz/½ bunch) watercress, leaves and tips only

½ small red onion, thinly sliced

35 g (1¼ oz/¼ cup) pistachio kernels coarsely chopped

SAUCE

15 g (½ oz) butter

1 small leek, white part only, thinly sliced

¼ teaspoondried mint

100 g (3½ oz/¾ cup) shelled peas

2 tablespoons chicken stock

50 g (1¾ oz) leaves and watercress tops of stems, chopped

a pinch cayenne pepper

2 tablespoons crème fraîche

1 **To make watercress sauce,** heat the butter in a medium frying pan over low heat and fry the leek for 5 minutes without browning. Add the mint and peas, cook for 1 minute and then add the stock. Bring to the boil, then reduce the heat and simmer for 5 minutes.

2 **Stir in the watercress,** increase the heat and simmer for 2 minutes, or until the liquid has evaporated. Add the cayenne and season with salt and pepper. Transfer to a food processor or blender and purée the sauce until very smooth. Return to the cleaned saucepan, stir in the crème fraîche and keep warm over a low heat. If necessary, stir in hot water, 1 teaspoon at a time, to maintain a thin mayonnaise consistency.

3 **Spray a barbecue grill** with olive oil. Lightly dust fish with flour and season with salt and freshly ground white pepper. Cook until opaque, 4–5 minutes each side, depending on the thickness of the fillets.

4 **Make a bed of watercress** on each serving plate. Scatter the red onion and pistachios over and around the watercress. Top with a fish fillet and spoon a dollop of sauce on each.

BARBECUED ASIAN-STYLE PRAWNS

SERVES 4

500 g (1 lb 2 oz) large raw prawns
   (shrimp)
lime wedges, to serve

MARINADE
2 tablespoons lemon juice
2 tablespoons sesame oil
2 garlic cloves, crushed
2 teaspoons grated fresh ginger

1   **Peel the prawns,** leaving the tails intact. Gently pull out the dark vein from each prawn back, starting from the head end.

2   **Mix the lemon juice,** sesame oil, garlic and ginger in a bowl. Add the prawns and gently stir to coat the prawns. Cover and refrigerate for at least 3 hours.

3   **Cook the prawns on a hot,** lightly oiled barbecue flatplate for 3–5 minutes, or until pink and cooked through. Brush frequently with marinade while cooking. Serve immediately with the lime wedges.

Notes: Alternatively, the prawns can be threaded onto bamboo skewers. Soak the skewers in cold water for about 30 minutes, or until they sink. This will prevent the skewers burning during cooking. After marinating, thread the prawns evenly onto the skewers and cook as stated, turning and basting occasionally during cooking.

The amount of garlic can be altered, according to taste. For a stronger flavour, double the quantity of garlic and omit the ginger.

For a spicy dish, substitute two finely chopped fresh chillies for the garlic. You can also halve the quantity of prawns and add scallops.

BARBECUED OCTOPUS

170 ml (5½ fl oz/⅔ cup) olive oil

10 g (¼ oz) chopped oregano

3 tablespoons chopped flat-leaf (Italian) parsley

1 tablespoon lemon juice

3 small red chillies, seeded and finely chopped

3 garlic cloves, crushed

1 kg (2 lb 4 oz) baby octopus

lime wedges, to serve

1   To make the marinade, combine the oil, herbs, lemon juice, chilli and garlic in a large bowl and mix well.

2   Use a small, sharp knife to remove the octopus heads. Grasp the bodies and push the beaks out from the centre with your index finger, then remove and discard. Slit the heads and remove the gut. If the octopus are too large, cut them into smaller portions.

3   Mix the octopus with the herb marinade. Cover and refrigerate for several hours, or overnight. Drain and reserve the marinade. Cook on a very hot, lightly oiled barbecue flatplate for 3–5 minutes, or until the flesh turns white. Turn frequently; brush generously with marinade during cooking.

CAJUN SWORDFISH

SERVES 4

1 tablespoon garlic powder

1 tablespoon onion powder

2 teaspoons white pepper

2 teaspoons cracked black pepper

2 teaspoons dried thyme

2 teaspoons dried oregano

1 teaspoon cayenne pepper

4 swordfish steaks

lime wedges, to serve

Greek-style yoghurt, to serve

mixed salad leaves, to serve

1 Mix all the dried spices and herbs in a bowl. Pat swordfish steaks dry with paper towels, then coat both sides of each one in the spice mixture, shaking off any excess.

2 Heat a barbecue flatplate and drizzle it with a little oil. Cook the swordfish steaks for 3–5 minutes on each side, depending on the thickness of each steak. Serve with wedges of lime, a dollop of yoghurt and a salad.

CAJUN PRAWNS WITH SALSA

SERVES 4

1.25 kg (2 lb 12 oz) large raw prawns (shrimp)

100 g (3½ oz) butter, melted

60 g (2¼ oz) watercress, washed and picked over

4 spring onions (scallions), chopped

lemon wedges, to serve

CAJUN SPICE MIX

1 tablespoon garlic powder

1 tablespoon onion powder

2 teaspoons dried thyme

2 teaspoons ground white pepper

1½ teaspoons cayenne pepper

½ teaspoon dried oregano

TOMATO SALSA

4 roma (plum) tomatoes, seeded and chopped

1 Lebanese (short) cucumber, peeled, seeded, chopped

2 tablespoons finely diced red onion

2 tablespoons chopped coriander (cilantro)

1 tablespoon chopped flat-leaf (Italian) parsley

1 garlic clove, crushed

2 tablespoons olive oil

1 tablespoon lime juice

1 **Combine all the ingredients** for the Cajun spice mix with 2 teaspoons cracked black pepper.

2 **To make the tomato salsa,** combine tomato, cucumber, onion, coriander and parsley in a bowl. Combine the garlic, oil and lime juice and season well. Add to the bowl; toss together.

3 **Peel and devein prawns,** leaving tails intact. Brush prawns with the butter and sprinkle generously with the spice mix. Cook on a barbecue flatplate, turning once, for 2–3 minutes each side, or until a crust forms and the prawns have turned pink and are cooked through.

4 **Lay some watercress on serving plates,** then spoon the salsa over the leaves. Arrange the prawns on top and sprinkle with some chopped spring onion. Serve with lemon wedges on the side.

BARBECUED CHICKEN WITH THAI STICKY RICE

SERVES 4–6

2 kg (4 lb 8 oz) chicken, cut into
  8–10 pieces

8 garlic cloves, chopped

6 coriander (cilantro) roots, chopped

1 large handful coriander (cilantro)
  leaves, chopped

1 tablespoon finely chopped fresh
  ginger

1 teaspoon ground white pepper

60 ml (2 fl oz/¼ cup) fish sauce

60 ml (2 fl oz/¼ cup) lime juice

60 ml (2 fl oz/¼ cup) whisky (optional)

600 g (1 lb 5 oz/3 cups) long-grain
  glutinous rice

cucumber slices, to serve

SAUCE

6 coriander (cilantro) roots, chopped

4 garlic cloves, chopped

2 bird's eye chillies, seeded and
  chopped

185 ml (6 fl oz/¾ cup) vinegar

4 tablespoons grated palm sugar
  (jaggery) or soft brown sugar

1 Put the chicken pieces in a non-metallic bowl. Combine the garlic, coriander root and leaves, ginger, white pepper and a pinch of salt and pound to a paste using a mortar and pestle. Mix in the fish sauce, lime juice and whisky (if using), then pour over the chicken and mix well. Marinate for at least 6 hours in the refrigerator. At the same time, soak rice for at least 3 hours in cold water.

2 To make the sauce, pound the coriander root, garlic, chilli and a pinch of salt to a paste using a mortar and pestle. Combine the vinegar, sugar and 185 ml (6 fl oz/¾ cup) water in a saucepan and stir until the sugar has dissolved. Bring to the boil, then add the paste and cook for 8–10 minutes, or until reduced by half. Set aside until ready to serve.

3 Drain the rice well, then line a bamboo steamer with muslin or banana leaves, spread rice over the top and cover with a tight-fitting lid. Steam over a wok or large saucepan of boiling water for 40 minutes, or until the rice is translucent, sticky and tender. If steam is escaping, wrap some foil over the top of the steamer. Keep covered until ready to serve.

4 Heat a barbecue flatplate to medium heat, then cook the chicken, turning regularly for about 25 minutes, or until tender and cooked through. The breast pieces may only take about 15 minutes so take them off first and keep warm.

5 Serve the chicken, rice, dipping sauce and cucumber on separate plates in the centre of the table and allow your guests to help themselves.

SERVES 4

2 teaspoons freshly cracked black pepper

2 teaspoons freshly cracked white pepper

1 teaspoon lightly crushed sea salt flakes

4 x 200 g (7 oz) eye fillet steaks

1 tablespoon olive oil

40 g (1½ oz) butter

2 large French shallots, finely chopped

1 garlic clove, crushed

2 tablespoons brandy

160 ml (5¼ fl oz/⅔ cup) beef stock

4 tablespoons thick (double/heavy) cream

1½ tablespoons green peppercorns in brine, drained and lightly crushed

2 teaspoons finely chopped flat-leaf (Italian) parsley

steamed asparagus, beans and new potatoes, to serve

1 Combine the black and white pepper with the sea salt flakes. Coat the steaks in the pepper mixture, patting it on to help adhere.

2 Preheat the barbecue flatplate to high heat and add the oil. Cook the steaks for 3–4 minutes on each side for medium–rare, or until cooked to your liking. Remove from the barbecue and cover to keep warm while you make the sauce.

3 Heat a frying pan over medium heat and add the butter, French shallots and garlic. Cook for 1 minute, or until softened. Remove from the heat, carefully add the brandy, then return to the heat. Bring to the boil, then add the beef stock, cream and green peppercorns and allow to come back to the boil. Cook for 3–4 minutes, or until glossy and thickened slightly, adding any juices from the resting steak. Add the parsley and season to taste. Serve the sauce over the steaks. Serve with asparagus, beans and potatoes.

BARBECUED FISH WITH ONIONS AND GINGER

SERVES 4

1 kg (2 lb 4 oz) small, firm whole snapper, scaled and gutted

2 teaspoons green peppercorns, drained and finely crushed

2 teaspoons finely chopped red chillies

3 teaspoons fish sauce

60 ml (2 fl oz/¼ cup) oil

2 onions, thinly sliced

4 cm (1½ inch) piece of ginger, thinly sliced

3 garlic cloves, cut into very thin slivers

2 teaspoons sugar

4 spring onions (scallions), finely shredded

LEMON AND GARLIC SAUCE

60 ml (2 fl oz/¼ cup) lemon juice

2 tablespoons fish sauce

1 tablespoon sugar

2 small red chillies, finely chopped

3 garlic cloves, chopped

1   **Wash the fish** and pat dry inside and out. Cut two or three diagonal slashes into the thickest part on both sides.

2   **Mix the peppercorns,** chillies and fish sauce to a paste and brush over the fish. Refrigerate for 20 minutes.

3   **Meanwhile, to make** the lemon and garlic sauce, stir the lemon juice, fish sauce, sugar, chilli and garlic in a bowl until the sugar has dissolved.

4   **Heat a barbecue flatplate** until very hot and brush with 1 tablespoon of oil. Cook the fish for 8 minutes on each side, or until the flesh flakes easily when tested with a fork.

5   **While the fish is cooking,** heat the remaining oil in a pan and stir the onion over medium heat for a few minutes, or until golden. Add the ginger, garlic and sugar and cook for another 3 minutes. Serve over the fish. Sprinkle with spring onion and serve with the sauce and steamed rice.

PIRI PIRI PRAWNS

SERVES 4

1 kg (2 lb 4 oz) large raw prawns (shrimp)

4 long red chillies, seeded

185 ml (6 fl oz/¾ cup) white wine vinegar

2 large garlic cloves, chopped

6–8 small red chillies, chopped

125 ml (4 fl oz/½ cup) olive oil

150 g (5½ oz) mixed lettuce leaves

1 **Remove the heads** from the prawns and slice them down the back without cutting right through, leaving the tail intact. Open out each prawn and remove the dark vein. Store the prepared prawns in the refrigerator while making the sauce.

2 **To make the sauce,** put the long chillies in a saucepan with the vinegar and simmer them over medium–high heat for 5 minutes, or until the chillies are soft. Let the mixture cool slightly, then put the chillies and 60 ml (2 fl oz/¼ cup) of the vinegar in a food processor. Add the garlic and chopped small chillies, and blend until the mixture is smooth. While the motor is running, gradually add the oil and remaining vinegar to the food processor.

3 **Put the prawns in the marinade,** making sure they are well coated, then cover them and refrigerate for 30 minutes.

4 **Remove prawns from the marinade,** bring the marinade to the boil and let it simmer for 5 minutes, or until it is slightly thickened and reduced. Take the prawns and the marinade out to the barbecue, and leave the saucepan with the marinade in it on the edge of the barbecue to keep warm.

5 **Lightly oil the barbecue grill** and heat it to high direct heat. Cook the prawns, basting them with the marinade, for 2–3 minutes on each side, or until they are cooked through. Arrange the lettuce on four plates, top it with the prawns and serve immediately with the chilli sauce.

CHILLI PORK RIBS

SERVES 4–6

1 kg (2 lb 4 oz) pork spareribs

125 g (4½ oz) tin puréed tomatoes

2 tablespoons honey

2 tablespoons chilli sauce

2 tablespoons hoisin sauce

2 tablespoons lime juice

2 garlic cloves, crushed

1 tablespoon oil

1 **Cut each rib into thirds**, then lay them in a single layer in a shallow non-metallic dish.

2 **Mix together all** the other ingredients except the oil and pour over the meat, turning to coat well. Cover with plastic wrap and refrigerate overnight, turning occasionally.

3 **Drain the ribs**, reserving the marinade, and cook them over medium heat on a lightly oiled barbecue grill or flatplate. Baste often with the marinade and cook for about 15–20 minutes, or until the ribs are tender and well browned, turning occasionally. Season to taste and serve immediately.

PORTUGUESE SPATCHCOCK

SERVES 4

1 red onion, chopped
6 garlic cloves, chopped
3 teaspoons grated lemon zest
2 teaspoons chilli flakes
1½ teaspoons paprika
60 ml (2 fl oz/¼ cup) oil
60 ml (2 fl oz/¼ cup) red wine vinegar
4 x 500 g (1 lb 2 oz) spatchcocks (poussin)
10 g (¼ oz/⅓ cup) chopped flat-leaf (Italian) parsley
lemon halves

1 Put the onion, garlic, lemon zest, chilli flakes, paprika, oil and vinegar in a food processor and blend them to a smooth paste.

2 Cut each of the spatchcocks down the backbone with sharp kitchen scissors and press down on the breastbone to flatten it out. Score the flesh and brush it with the spice mixture, then put the spatchcocks in a non-metallic dish, cover and refrigerate overnight.

3 Preheat the barbecue grill to low–medium direct heat. Grill the spatchcocks for 10 minutes on each side, or until they are cooked through (test by piercing the thigh with a skewer — if the juices run clear, they are ready), then sprinkle with parsley and serve with the lemon halves.

Note: Try grilling the lemon halves briefly to bring out a bit of extra flavour.

ROSEMARY AND PEPPER RIB-EYE STEAKS WITH MASH

SERVES 4

4 tablespoons roughly chopped rosemary

4 tablespoons freshly ground black pepper

250 ml (9 fl oz/1 cup) olive oil

4 rib-eye steaks

OLIVE OIL MASH

750 g (1 lb 10 oz) potatoes

4 tablespoons extra virgin olive oil

1 garlic clove, chopped

125 ml (4 fl oz/½ cup) cream

1   Combine the rosemary, pepper and oil in a large shallow non-metallic dish. Add the steaks, turn to coat well on both sides, then cover and refrigerate overnight.

2   Preheat a barbecue flatplate or grill to medium. Meanwhile, boil, steam or microwave the potatoes until tender.

3   Drain the steaks and cook them on the flatplate for about 10 minutes on each side for medium rare, or until cooked to your liking — the exact cooking time will vary depending on the thickness of your steaks. Take them off the heat, cover loosely with foil and allow to rest for 5 minutes.

4   While the steaks are resting, make the olive oil mash. Drain the hot, cooked potatoes, then put them in a large bowl and mash them. Gently heat the oil and garlic in a small pan until the garlic starts to sizzle and soften. Take the pan off the heat and strain the oil, discarding the garlic. Meanwhile, heat the cream in another small pan until just hot. Gradually beat the warm garlic oil into the mashed potato and then add enough cream to give a soft texture. Season to taste with salt and cracked black pepper. Serve hot with the rib-eye steaks.

FILLET STEAK WITH FLAVOURED BUTTERS

SERVES 4

4 fillet steaks

CAPSICUM BUTTER

1 small red capsicum (pepper)

125 g (4½ oz) butter

2 teaspoons chopped oregano

2 teaspoons chopped chives

GARLIC BUTTER

125 g (4½ oz) butter

3 garlic cloves, crushed

2 spring onions (scallions), finely chopped

1 **Cut a pocket** in each steak.

2 **For the capsicum butter,** cut the capsicum into large pieces and place, skin-side up, under a hot grill (broiler) until the skin blisters and blackens. Put in a plastic bag until cool, then peel away the skin and dice the flesh.

3 **Beat the butter until creamy.** Add the capsicum, oregano and chives, season and beat until smooth.

4 **For the garlic butter,** beat the butter until creamy, add the garlic and spring onion and beat until smooth.

5 **Push capsicum butter** into the pockets in two of the steaks and garlic butter into the other two. Cook on a hot, lightly oiled barbecue grill or flatplate for 4–5 minutes each side, turning once. Brush frequently with any remaining flavoured butter while cooking. These steaks are delicious served with a simple green salad.

VEAL STACKS WITH MOZZARELLA

SERVES 4

1 small eggplant (aubergine)

125 g (4½ oz/½ cup) tomato passata (puréed tomatoes)

1 garlic clove, crushed

¼ teaspoon sugar

oil, for brushing

4 x 150 g (5½ oz) butterflied veal loin steaks

50 g (1¾ oz) baby rocket (arugula) leaves

75 g (2½ oz/½ cup) coarsely grated mozzarella cheese

1 **Slice the eggplant** into 5 mm (¼ inch) thick rounds. Put them in a colander and sprinkle generously with salt to draw out the juice. Leave for 20 minutes, then rinse well under cold running water and pat dry with paper towels.

2 **Put the passata,** garlic and sugar in a small bowl. Season to taste and set aside.

3 **Preheat a barbecue grill** or flatplate to high. Brush both sides of each eggplant slice with a little oil and cook for about 15 minutes, turning once, or until lightly browned on both sides. Remove from the heat.

4 **Brush the veal steaks** with a little oil, season with salt and pepper, then cook on the flatplate for about 3–5 minutes on each side, or until nicely browned and cooked to your liking. Remove from the heat.

5 **Arrange the rocket,** eggplant slices, passata mixture and mozzarella on top of each steak. Put the steaks under a hot grill (broiler) and cook for 1 minute, or until the cheese is golden. Serve hot.

STEAKS FILLED WITH BOCCONCINI AND TOMATO

SERVES 6

6 New York style (boneless sirloin) steaks

200 g (7 oz) semi-dried (sun-blushed) tomatoes, chopped

200 g (7 oz) bocconcini (fresh baby mozzarella) cheese, chopped

2 garlic cloves, crushed

2 tablespoons finely chopped flat-leaf (Italian) parsley

oil, for brushing

1 **Cut a slit along the side** of each steak to form a pocket. Combine the tomato, bocconcini, garlic and parsley in a small bowl with a little salt and pepper. Fill each steak with the mixture and secure with toothpicks to hold the filling in.

2 **Preheat a barbecue grill** to medium. Just before cooking, brush the steaks lightly with oil and season with salt and pepper. Cook the steaks for 3–4 minutes on each side for medium rare, or until cooked to your liking, turning only once. Remove the toothpicks and serve with vegetables or a salad.

Note: You can fill the steaks ahead of time — simply keep them covered in the refrigerator. Bring to room temperature just before you're ready to cook.

HOISIN LAMB WITH CHARRED SPRING ONION

SERVES 4

800 g (1 lb 12 oz) lamb loin

60 ml (2 fl oz/¼ cup) hoisin sauce

2 tablespoons soy sauce

2 garlic cloves, bruised

1 tablespoon grated fresh ginger

2 teaspoons olive oil

16 spring onions (scallions), trimmed to 18 cm (7 inches) long

40 g (1½ oz/¼ cup) chopped toasted peanuts

1   **Trim the lamb** of any excess fat and sinew. Combine the hoisin sauce, soy sauce, garlic, ginger and 1 teaspoon of the oil in a shallow dish, add the lamb and turn it so that it is well coated in the marinade. Cover the dish and refrigerate for 4 hours or overnight.

2   **Toss the trimmed spring onions** with the remaining oil and season them well. Remove the lamb from the marinade, season the meat and pour the marinade into a small saucepan. Simmer the marinade for 5 minutes, or until slightly reduced.

3   **Preheat a barbecue grill** or flatplate to medium direct heat. Cook lamb for 5–6 minutes on each side, or until it is cooked to your liking, brushing it frequently with the reduced marinade, then let it rest, covered, for 3 minutes. Cook the spring onions for 1–2 minutes, or until they are tender, but still firm.

4   **Cut the lamb** across the grain into 2 cm (¾ inch) thick slices, and arrange it on a serving plate. Drizzle any juices that have been released during resting over the lamb and sprinkle it with the toasted peanuts. Serve with the spring onions.

FIVE-SPICE ROAST CHICKEN

SERVES 4

1.8 kg (4 lb) chicken

1 tablespoon soy sauce

2 garlic cloves, crushed

1 teaspoon finely grated ginger

1 tablespoon honey

1 tablespoon rice wine

1 teaspoon five-spice

1 tablespoon peanut oil

1 Wash the chicken and pat it thoroughly dry inside and out with paper towels. Whisk the soy sauce, garlic, ginger, honey, rice wine and five-spice together in a small bowl and brush it all over the chicken, ensuring every bit of skin is well coated. Put the chicken on a wire rack over a baking tray and refrigerate it, uncovered, for at least 8 hours, or overnight.

2 Preheat a kettle or covered barbecue to medium indirect heat and put a drip tray under the rack. Brush the chicken liberally with the peanut oil and put it breast-side up in the middle of the barbecue over the drip tray. Cover the barbecue and roast the chicken for 1 hour 10 minutes, or until the juices run clear when you pierce it with a skewer between the thigh and body. Check the chicken every so often, and if it appears to be over-browning, cover it loosely with foil. Leave it to rest, covered, for 10 minutes before carving and serving. The flavours in this style of chicken go particularly well with steamed Asian greens and fried rice.

TUNA STEAKS WITH SALSA AND GARLIC MASH

SERVES 4

4 tuna steaks (about 150 g/5½ oz each)

olive oil, for brushing

sea salt

GARLIC MASH

1 kg (2 lb 4 oz) floury (starchy) potatoes, cut into chunks

6–8 garlic cloves, peeled

80 ml (2½ fl oz/⅓ cup) milk

60 ml (2 fl oz/¼ cup) olive oil

SALSA

1 tablespoon olive oil

2 French shallots, finely chopped

200 g (7 oz) green olives, pitted and quartered lengthways

35 g (1½ oz/¼ cup) currants, soaked in warm water for 10 minutes

1 tablespoon baby capers, rinsed and squeezed dry

1 tablespoon sherry vinegar

2 tablespoons shredded mint leaves

1 **Boil the potato chunks** and garlic for 10–15 minutes, or until tender. Drain them, then return the pan to the heat, shaking it to evaporate any excess water. Remove the pan from the heat and mash the potato and garlic until smooth, then stir in the milk and olive oil, and season with salt and freshly ground black pepper.

2 **To make the salsa,** heat oil in a frying pan over medium heat. Cook shallots for 2–4 minutes, or until they are softened, but not browned, then add the olives, drained currants and capers. Cook for 2 minutes, stirring continuously. Add vinegar and cook for 2 minutes, or until the liquid is reduced by about half. Remove the pan from the heat and keep the salsa warm until you're ready to dish up.

3 **Preheat a barbecue grill** or flatplate to medium–high direct heat. Brush the tuna steaks with olive oil, season them well with sea salt and freshly ground black pepper, and grill for 2–3 minutes each side for medium–rare, or until they are cooked to your liking. Stir the mint into the salsa and serve it immediately with the garlic mash and tuna.

SPICY WHOLE SNAPPER WITH A WINE BUTTER SAUCE

SERVES 4

1 kg (2 lb 4 oz) whole snapper, cleaned and scaled

2 celery stalks, sliced on the diagonal

2 red capsicums (peppers), sliced on the diagonal

3 spring onions (scallions), thinly sliced

125 ml (4 fl oz/½ cup) white wine

1 tablespoon shichimi togarashi or nanami togarashi seasoning (from Japanese supermarkets)

1 lemon, halved lengthways and thinly sliced

40 g (1½ oz) unsalted butter, chopped

1 **Preheat a kettle** or covered barbecue to medium indirect heat.

2 **Trim the snapper fins** using a pair of kitchen scissors. Wash the fish well and pat dry with paper towels. Take two sheets of foil large enough to encase the fish and lay them on a flat surface. Top with the same amount of baking paper. Fold the edges into a tight, secure seam to form a large waterproof casing for the fish.

3 **Spread the celery,** capsicum and spring onion in the centre of the baking paper, then lay the fish lengthways over the vegetables. Pour the wine over and around the fish and sprinkle generously with salt, freshly ground black pepper and the Japanese seasoning. Overlap the lemon slices along the centre of the fish, then dot with butter and enclose the paper over the fish. Fold the ends in several times to seal in the liquid.

4 **Put the fish parcel** on the barbecue grill, then lower the lid and cook for about 15 minutes, or until the fish flakes when tested in the thickest part with a fork. Serve hot, with rice and lightly steamed green vegetables.

STUFFED PORK CHOPS WITH SPRING ONIONS

SERVES 6

2 tablespoons dry sherry

4 dried dessert figs

1 tablespoon butter

60 ml (2 fl oz/¼ cup) olive oil

1 small onion, finely diced

2 garlic cloves, crushed

1 large granny smith apple, peeled, cored and grated

2 tablespoons slivered almonds, lightly toasted

1 tablespoon finely chopped sage leaves

6 large pork loin chops (250 g/9 oz each) on the bone

16 large bulb spring onions (scallions), green parts removed, halved

1 **Bring the sherry** and 1 tablespoon of water to the boil in a small saucepan. Soak the figs in the hot sherry mixture for about 20 minutes, then slice them finely and keep the soaking liquid to use later.

2 **Heat the butter** and 1 tablespoon of olive oil in a frying pan, add the onion and garlic, and cook over low heat for 5 minutes or until they are softened. Add the grated apple, figs and sherry liquid, and simmer for a further 5 minutes, or until the apple has softened and most of the liquid has evaporated. Remove the pan from the heat and stir in the almonds and sage, then season well and allow the mixture to cool.

3 **Trim the pork chops** of any excess fat and make an incision into the middle of the chop from the side. Be careful — you only want to make a pocket in the flesh and not cut right through.

4 **Fill the pocket with the apple** and fig stuffing, pushing it well into the cavity so that none is spilling out — you should fit about 1½ tablespoons of filling in each chop. Brush chops all over with 1 tablespoon of the olive oil, and season with salt and freshly ground black pepper. Toss the spring onion with the remaining oil, and season it well.

5 **Heat a barbecue grill or flatplate** to medium direct heat. Cook chops for 8 minutes on each side, or until the outside is slightly charred and the meat is cooked through. While the chops are cooking, add spring onions to the chargrill plate and cook for 10 minutes, or until softened. Serve the chops and spring onions as soon as they come off the barbecue.

LAMB CHOPS WITH CITRUS POCKETS

4 lamb chump chops, about 250 g
(9 oz) each

2 tablespoons lemon juice

CITRUS FILLING

3 spring onions (scallions), finely
chopped

1 celery stalk, finely chopped

2 teaspoons grated fresh ginger

60 g (2¼ oz/¾ cup) fresh breadcrumbs

2 tablespoons orange juice

2 teaspoons finely grated orange zest

1 teaspoon chopped rosemary

1   Cut a deep, long pocket in the side of each lamb chop. Mix together the spring onion, celery, ginger, breadcrumbs, orange juice, zest and rosemary and spoon into the pockets in the lamb.

2   Cook on a hot, lightly oiled barbecue flatplate or grill, turning once, for 15 minutes, or until the lamb is cooked through but still pink in the centre. Drizzle with the lemon juice before serving.

KING PRAWNS WITH DILL MAYONNAISE

SERVES 4

16–20 raw king prawns (shrimp)

MARINADE

125 ml (4 fl oz/½ cup) olive oil

80 ml (2½ fl oz/⅓ cup) lemon juice

2 tablespoons wholegrain mustard

2 tablespoons honey

2 tablespoons chopped dill

DILL MAYONNAISE

185 g (6½ oz/¾ cup) mayonnaise

2 tablespoons chopped dill

1½ tablespoons lemon juice

1 gherkin, finely chopped

1 teaspoon chopped capers

1 garlic clove, crushed

1 **To make the marinade,** combine the olive oil, lemon juice, mustard, honey and dill, pour over the unpeeled prawns and coat well. Cover and refrigerate for at least 2 hours, turning occasionally.

2 **To make dill mayonnaise,** whisk the mayonnaise, dill, lemon juice, gherkin, capers and garlic. Cover and refrigerate.

3 **Cook the drained prawns on a hot,** lightly oiled barbecue grill or flatplate in batches for 4 minutes, turning frequently until pink and cooked through. Serve with the mayonnaise.

MALAYSIAN BARBECUED SEAFOOD

SERVES 4

1 onion, grated

4 garlic cloves, chopped

5 cm (2 inch) piece of ginger, grated

3 stems lemon grass (white part only), chopped

2 teaspoons ground or grated fresh turmeric

1 teaspoon shrimp paste

80 ml (2½ fl oz/⅓ cup) vegetable oil

¼ teaspoon salt

4 calamari tubes

2 thick white boneless fish fillets

8 raw king prawns (shrimp)

banana leaves, to serve

2 limes, cut into wedges

strips of lime zest, to garnish

mint leaves, to garnish

1 **Combine the onion,** garlic, ginger, lemon grass, turmeric, shrimp paste, oil and salt in a small food processor. Process in short bursts until the mixture forms a paste.

2 **Cut calamari** in half lengthways and lay it on the bench with the soft inside facing up. Score a very fine honeycomb pattern into the soft side, taking care not to cut all the way through, and then cut into large pieces. Wash all the seafood under cold running water; pat dry with paper towels. Brush lightly with the spice paste, then place on a tray, cover and refrigerate for 15 minutes.

3 **Lightly oil a barbecue grill** or flatplate and heat. When the plate is hot, arrange the fish fillets and prawns on the plate. Cook, turning once only, for about 3 minutes each side or until the fish flesh is just firm and the prawns turn bright pink to orange. Add calamari pieces and cook for about 2 minutes or until the flesh turns white and rolls up. Take care not to overcook the seafood.

4 **Arrange the seafood** on a platter lined with the banana leaves, add the lime wedges and serve immediately, garnished with strips of lime zest and some fresh mint.

LEMON AND SAGE VEAL CHOPS WITH ROCKET

SERVES 4

4 veal chops

2 tablespoons olive oil

1 tablespoon lemon juice

4 strips lemon zest

10 g (¼ oz) roughly chopped sage leaves

3 garlic cloves, peeled and bruised

lemon wedges, to serve

ROCKET SALAD

100 g (3½ oz) rocket (arugula), washed and picked

1 avocado, sliced

1½ tablespoons extra virgin olive oil

2 teaspoons balsamic vinegar

1 **Trim any fat and sinew** from the chops and put them in a shallow, non-metallic dish with the olive oil, lemon juice, lemon zest, sage and garlic. Turn the chops so that they are evenly coated, then season them with freshly ground black pepper, cover and refrigerate for 4 hours or preferably overnight.

2 **Put the rocket** in a large serving bowl and scatter the avocado over it. Drizzle the olive oil and balsamic vinegar over the salad, season it with a little salt and ground black pepper and toss gently.

3 **Preheat a barbecue grill or flatplate** to medium–high direct heat. Remove the chops from the marinade, season well with salt and chargrill them for 5–6 minutes on each side, or until cooked to your liking. Remove the chops from the barbecue, cover them loosely with foil and let them rest for 5 minutes.

4 **Put the chops** on a serving dish, drizzle them with any juices that have been released while they rested and serve with the rocket salad and lemon wedges.

LAMB KOFTA WITH BABA GHANOUSH AND OLIVES

SERVES 4

1 tablespoon chopped flat-leaf (Italian) parsley
½ teaspoon sumac
200 g (7 oz) Kalamata olives
olive oil, for brushing
4 pieces pitta bread
baba ghanoush, to serve
tabouleh, to serve

KOFTA

1 red onion, finely chopped
25 g (1 oz) chopped flat-leaf (Italian) parsley
25 g (1 oz) chopped coriander (cilantro) leaves
15 g (½ oz) chopped mint leaves
1 tablespoon paprika
1 tablespoon ground cumin
1½ teaspoons allspice
½ teaspoon ground ginger
½ teaspoon chilli flakes
1.2 kg (2 lb 11 oz) minced (ground) lamb
60 ml (2 fl oz/¼ cup) soda water

1 **To make the kofta,** put the onion, parsley, coriander, mint, paprika, cumin, allspice, ginger and chilli in a food processor and blend until they are combined. Season the mixture with 2 teaspoons salt and some freshly ground black pepper, then add the minced lamb to the food processor and get the motor going again. Add soda water in a thin stream until the mixture forms a smooth paste, then cover and refrigerate for at least 2 hours, or preferably overnight.

2 **Soak four wooden skewers** in cold water for 1 hour. Divide the lamb mixture into 12 portions and mould each portion into a torpedo shape, using damp hands to stop the meat from sticking to them. Then cover and refrigerate the kofta. Thread the olives onto the soaked skewers.

3 **When ready to cook the kofta,** preheat a barbecue flatplate to medium–high direct heat. Brush the kofta lightly with olive oil and cook, turning frequently, for 10–12 minutes, or until they are evenly browned and cooked through. When the kofta are nearly cooked, add the olives to the barbecue for 1–2 minutes. Serve the kofta immediately with pitta bread, baba ghanoush, tabouleh and grilled olives.

CHICKEN WITH SALSA VERDE

SERVES 6

1 garlic clove

4 heaped tablespoons fresh flat-leaf (Italian) parsley

80 ml (2¼ fl oz/⅓ cup) extra virgin olive oil

3 tablespoons chopped dill

1½ tablespoons Dijon mustard

1 tablespoon sherry vinegar

1 tablespoon baby capers, drained

6 large chicken breast fillets

1 **Place the garlic,** parsley, olive oil, dill, mustard, vinegar and capers in a food processor or a blender and process until almost smooth.

2 **Cook the chicken fillets** on a very hot, lightly oiled barbecue grill or flatplate for 4–5 minutes each side, or until cooked through.

3 **Cut each chicken fillet** into three on the diagonal and arrange on serving plates. Top with a spoonful of salsa verde and season to taste.

MARINATED LAMB

SERVES 4

15 g (½ oz) finely chopped flat-leaf (Italian) parsley

20 g (¾ oz) finely chopped coriander (cilantro) leaves

4 garlic cloves, crushed

1 tablespoon paprika

1 teaspoon dried thyme

125 ml (4 fl oz/½ cup) olive oil

60 ml (2 fl oz/¼ cup) lemon juice

2 teaspoons ground cumin

4 x 250 g (9 oz) lamb rumps or pieces of tenderloin, trimmed

1 Mix the parsley, coriander, garlic, paprika, thyme, oil, lemon juice and 1½ teaspoons cumin together in a non-metallic dish. Score diagonal lines in the fat on lamb pieces with a sharp knife, then put them in the marinade, turning so they are evenly coated. Cover and refrigerate for at least 2 hours or overnight.

2 Heat a barbecue flatplate to medium direct heat. Season the lamb to taste with white pepper, the remaining ½ teaspoon of cumin and some salt. Cook the rumps fat-side up for 3 minutes and then cook the other side for 2–3 minutes, making sure the fat is well cooked. Take the lamb off the barbecue as soon as it is done, cover it with foil and put it aside to rest for about 5 minutes before carving.

SWEET CHILLI OCTOPUS

SERVES 4

1.5 kg (3 lb 5 oz) baby octopus
250 ml (9 fl oz/1 cup) sweet chilli sauce
80 ml (2½ fl oz/⅓ cup) lime juice
80 ml (2½ fl oz/⅓ cup) fish sauce
60 g (2¼ oz/⅓ cup) soft brown sugar
lime wedges, to serve

1 **Cut off the octopus heads,** below the eyes, with a sharp knife. Discard heads and guts. Push the beaks out with your index finger, remove and discard. Wash the octopus thoroughly under running water and drain on crumpled paper towels. If the octopus tentacles are large, cut into quarters.

2 **Combine sweet chilli sauce,** juice, fish sauce and sugar.

3 **Cook the octopus on a very hot,** lightly oiled barbecue grill or flatplate, turning often, for 3–4 minutes, or until it just changes colour. Brush with a quarter of the sauce during cooking. Take care not to overcook the octopus or it will toughen. Serve immediately with the remaining sauce and lime wedges.

SQUID WITH PICADA DRESSING

SERVES 6

500 g (1 lb 2 oz) small squid

¼ teaspoon salt

PICADA DRESSING

2 tablespoons extra virgin olive oil

2 tablespoons finely chopped flat-leaf (Italian) parsley

1 garlic clove, crushed

¼ teaspoon cracked black pepper

1 To clean the squid, gently pull the tentacles away from the hood (the intestines should come away at the same time). Remove the intestines from the tentacles by cutting under the eyes, then remove the beak, if it remains in the centre of the tentacles, by pushing up with your index finger. Pull away the soft bone.

2 Rub the hoods under cold running water and the skin should come away easily. Wash the hoods and tentacles and drain well. Place in a bowl, add the salt and mix well. Cover and refrigerate for about 30 minutes.

3 For the picada dressing, whisk together the olive oil, parsley, garlic, pepper and some salt.

4 Cook squid hoods in small batches on a very hot, lightly oiled barbecue flatplate for 2–3 minutes, or until white and tender. Barbecue or grill the squid tentacles, turning to brown them all over, for 1 minute, or until they curl up. Serve hot, drizzled with the picada dressing.

BLACKENED CAJUN SPICED CHICKEN

SERVES 4

1½ tablespoons onion powder

1½ tablespoons garlic powder

2 teaspoons paprika

1 teaspoon white pepper

2 teaspoons dried thyme

½–1 teaspoon chilli powder

1 teaspoon salt

8 chicken drumsticks, scored

1 **Combine the onion powder,** garlic powder, paprika, white pepper, thyme, chilli powder and salt in a plastic bag. Place the drumsticks in the bag and shake until all the pieces are coated. Leave the chicken in the fridge for at least 30 minutes to allow the flavours to develop, or overnight if time permits.

2 **Cook chicken** on a lightly oiled barbecue grill or flatplate for about 1 hour, or until it is slightly blackened and cooked through. Brush lightly with some oil to prevent drying out during cooking.

CHILLI LAMB CHOPS

SERVES 4

4 garlic cloves, crushed
1 tablespoon grated ginger
1 teaspoon vegetable oil
1 teaspoon sambal oelek
2 teaspoons ground coriander
2 teaspoons ground cumin
2 tablespoons soy sauce
2 teaspoons sesame oil
2 tablespoons sweet chilli sauce
2 tablespoons lemon juice
12 lamb chops

1 **Combine the garlic,** ginger, oil, sambal oelek, coriander, cumin, soy sauce, sesame oil, sweet chili sauce, and lemon juice in a bowl. Season with salt and cracked black pepper.

2 **Place the chops** in a nonmetallic dish and pour the marinade on top, coating all sides. Allow to marinate for 20 minutes.

3 **Cook the chops** on a very hot barbecue flatplate or grill for 3 minutes each side or until cooked to your liking. Serve with steamed rice.

LEMON AND HERB RAINBOW TROUT

SERVES 4

3 tablespoons chopped dill

2 tablespoons chopped rosemary

4 tablespoons roughly chopped flat-leaf (Italian) parsley

2 teaspoons thyme

1½ tablespoons green peppercorns, drained and crushed

80 ml (2½ fl oz/⅓ cup) lemon juice

1 lemon, sliced, plus some extra slices, for garnish (optional)

4 whole rainbow trout, scaled and gutted

80 ml (2½ fl oz/⅓ cup) dry white wine

HORSERADISH CREAM

1 tablespoon horseradish cream

125 g (4½ oz/½ cup) sour cream

2 tablespoons cream

LEMON SAUCE

150 g (5½ oz) butter

2 egg yolks

3–4 tablespoons lemon juice

1 Cut eight sheets of foil large enough to wrap the fish in. Lay four of them out on a flat surface, then put a second sheet on each piece so that each piece is a double thickness. Lightly grease the top sheets.

2 Heat a barbecue. Mix the herbs, peppercorns, juice and salt and freshly ground black pepper, to taste, in a bowl. Put a few slices of lemon in each fish cavity. Wipe any slime off the fish with paper towel. Spoon the herb mixture into the fish cavities.

3 Lay each fish onto a piece of foil and sprinkle each with 1 tablespoon of wine. Fold the foil to form parcels. Cook on the barbecue for about 15 minutes, or until the fish is just cooked through.

4 Leave the wrapped fish for 5 minutes, then serve with horseradish cream and lemon sauce.

5 For the horseradish cream, mix the creams in a bowl and season with salt and pepper, to taste.

6 For the lemon sauce, melt the butter in a small saucepan over low heat, without stirring. Skim the foam off the surface and pour off the clear yellow liquid, leaving the milky sediment behind. Discard the sediment. Blend the egg yolks in a food processor for 20 seconds. With the motor running, add the butter slowly in a thin, steady stream. Continue processing until all the butter has been added and the mixture is thick and creamy. Add the lemon juice and season with salt and pepper. Garnish the fish with barbecued lemon slices and perhaps some strips of chives.

CHARGRILLED JUMBO PRAWNS

SERVES 4

8 large raw king prawns (800 g/
    1 lb 12 oz)

80 ml (2½ fl oz/⅓ cup) olive oil

3 garlic cloves, crushed

1 tablespoon sweet chilli sauce

2 tablespoons lime juice

60 ml (2 fl oz/¼ cup) olive oil, extra

2 tablespoons lime juice, extra

mixed lettuce leaves, to serve

1 **Remove the heads** from the prawns and, using a sharp knife, cut through the centre of the prawns lengthways to form two halves, leaving the tails and shells intact.

2 **Place the olive oil,** 2 crushed garlic cloves, sweet chilli sauce and lime juice in a large bowl, and combine well. Add the prawns, toss to coat and marinate for 30 minutes.

3 **Meanwhile, combine extra oil** and lime juice and the remaining garlic in a bowl. Heat a barbecue grill or flatplate until hot. Drain prawns and cook cut-side-down first, brushing with the marinade, for 1–2 minutes each side, or until cooked. Divide lettuce among four serving plates, place prawns on top and spoon over the dressing. Season and serve.

CHINESE-STYLE BARBECUE SPARERIBS

SERVES 6

60 ml (2 fl oz/¼ cup) hoisin sauce

80 ml (2½ fl oz/⅓ cup) oyster sauce

2 tablespoons rice wine

125 ml (4 fl oz/½ cup) soy sauce

6 garlic cloves, crushed

3 teaspoons finely grated fresh ginger

2 kg (4 lb 8 oz) American-style pork ribs

2 tablespoons honey

1 Mix the hoisin sauce, oyster sauce, rice wine, soy sauce, garlic and ginger in a large, non-metallic bowl, add the ribs and turn them so that they are coated in the marinade. Cover the bowl and refrigerate for at least 4 hours, or overnight.

2 Remove the ribs from the marinade and tip the marinade into a small saucepan with the honey. Simmer the mixture over low heat for 5 minutes, or until it becomes slightly syrupy — you will be using this to baste the ribs as they cook.

3 Heat a kettle or covered barbecue to medium indirect heat and cook the ribs, covered, for 10 minutes, then turn them over and cook them for another 5 minutes. Continue cooking, basting and turning the ribs frequently for 30 minutes, or until they are cooked through and caramelized all over.

4 Once the ribs are cooked, let them rest, covered, for 10 minutes, then cut the racks into individual ribs to serve. Make sure there are plenty of napkins available — these ribs should be eaten with your fingers and are deliciously sticky.

MARINATED BEEF RIBS IN DARK ALE AND MUSTARD

SERVES 4

4 beef spare ribs (total weight about 2 kg/4 lb 8 oz), halved

125 ml (4 fl oz/½ cup) dark ale beer

2 tablespoons soft brown sugar

3 tablespoons cider vinegar

2 small red chillies, seeded and finely chopped

2 tablespoons ground cumin

1 tablespoon seeded mustard

20 g (¾ oz) unsalted butter

1   Arrange the ribs in a shallow non-metallic dish. Put the ale, sugar, vinegar, chilli, cumin and mustard in a large bowl, stir well to dissolve the sugar and pour over the ribs. Toss to coat, then cover and marinate in the refrigerator for 1–2 hours.

2   Preheat a kettle or covered barbecue to medium indirect heat. Put the ribs in a large shallow roasting tin and place it in the middle of the barbecue. Lower the lid and cook for 50 minutes, or until meat is tender and about 125 ml (4 fl oz/ ½ cup) of liquid is left in the roasting tin. Transfer the ribs to a serving plate.

3   While the barbecue is still hot, put the roasting tin with all its juices over direct heat to warm through. Using a whisk, beat in the butter and season with salt and freshly ground black pepper. Arrange the ribs on four serving plates and drizzle with the warm sauce. Serve with baked potatoes and steamed greens.

LAMB CUTLETS WITH ONION MARMALADE

SERVES 4

2 tablespoons butter

80 ml (2½ fl oz/⅓ cup) olive oil

4 onions, finely sliced

2 teaspoons brown sugar

2 teaspoons thyme leaves

2 tablespoons parsley, finely chopped

12 French-trimmed lamb cutlets

2 tablespoons lemon juice

1 Heat butter and half the olive oil together in a saucepan. Add onion, sugar and thyme and stir well. Turn heat to low, cover the saucepan and cook the onion, stirring occasionally for 30 –35 minutes, or until it is very soft and golden. Season well, stir in parsley and keep warm over a very low heat.

2 Heat remaining oil on a barbecue flatplate and, when hot, add cutlets in a single layer. Cook for 2 minutes on each side, or until the lamb is browned on the outside but still feels springy when you press it. Add lemon juice and season well.

3 Put a small pile of the onion and herb marmalade on each plate and place the cutlets around it.

PORK AND POLENTA STACK

SERVES 4

1.125 litres (39 fl oz/4½ cups) chicken stock

2 teaspoons balsamic vinegar

1 teaspoon Worcestershire sauce

1 teaspoon cornflour (cornstarch)

150 g (5½ oz/1 cup) instant polenta

2 tablespoons grated parmesan cheese

oil, for brushing

2 x 200 g (7 oz) pork fillets

chopped flat-leaf (Italian) parsley, to serve

1 **In a small saucepan,** combine 185 ml (6 fl oz/¾ cup) of the stock with the vinegar, Worcestershire sauce and cornflour. Stir over medium heat until the mixture boils and thickens, then set aside.

2 **In another saucepan,** bring the remaining stock to the boil. Add the polenta and stir constantly over medium heat for 7 minutes, or until the mixture has thickened and the polenta is soft. Stir in the parmesan, and some salt and pepper to taste. Pour into a lightly oiled 23 cm (9 inch) square cake tin and allow to cool. Refrigerate for 1 hour, or until firm.

3 **Preheat a barbecue grill** or flatplate to medium. Turn the polenta out of the tin and cut it into four squares. Lightly brush both sides with oil and cook for 3–4 minutes on each side, or until golden all over. Set aside and keep warm.

4 **Cut each pork fillet** in half crossways. Place between two sheets of plastic wrap and rest cut-side-down on a chopping board, then gently flatten them slightly with a rolling pin or mallet. Brush the flatplate with a little more oil and cook the pork for 4 minutes on each side, or until just cooked through. Meanwhile, reheat the sauce.

5 **Divide the polenta** among four serving plates and top with a slice of pork. Drizzle with the warm sauce, sprinkle with parsley and serve with mixed vegetables.

REDFISH IN CORN HUSKS WITH CAPSICUM SALAD

SERVES 6

6 small red mullet, scaled and gutted

12 lemon thyme sprigs

1 lemon, sliced

2 garlic cloves, sliced

12 large corn husks

olive oil, for drizzling

2 bunches asparagus, trimmed

lemon wedges, to serve

SALAD

1 red capsicum (pepper)

2 tablespoons virgin olive oil

1 small garlic clove, crushed

1 tablespoon lemon juice

1 tablespoon chopped basil

1 tablespoon pine nuts

100 g (3½ oz/½ cup) small black olives

1 **To make the salad,** cut the capsicum into large pieces. Put skin-side up under a hot griller (broiler) until skin blackens and blisters. Alternatively, hold over the coals or gas flame of a barbecue. Cool in a plastic bag, then peel off the skin. Finely dice the flesh.

2 **Combine the olive oil,** garlic, lemon juice and basil in a small bowl and whisk together. Add the capsicum, pine nuts and olives.

3 **Wash the fish** and pat dry inside and out with paper towels. Fill each fish cavity with thyme, lemon and garlic, then place each in a corn husk. Drizzle with oil and sprinkle with pepper, then top each fish with another husk. Tie each end of the husks with string to enclose.

4 **Place on coals** or on a barbecue flatplate and cook, turning once, for 6–8 minutes, or until the fish is cooked and flakes easily when tested with a fork. A few minutes after you've started cooking the fish, brush asparagus with oil and cook, turning occasionally, on the barbecue for 3–4 minutes, or until tender. Pour dressing over the asparagus and serve with the fish and salad.

BARBECUED STEAK WITH CARAMELIZED ONIONS

SERVES 4

2 capsicums (peppers), 1 red and
  1 yellow, seeded and quartered

2 zucchini (courgettes), trimmed and
  sliced lengthways into strips

2 tablespoons oil

2 large red onions, thinly sliced

4 rump steaks (about 200 g/7 oz each)

2 tablespoons soft brown sugar

60 ml (2 fl oz/¼ cup) balsamic vinegar

CRÈME FRAÎCHE

1½ tablespoons wholegrain mustard

200 g (7 oz) crème fraîche

1 Heat a barbecue flatplate or grill to hot. Combine the mustard and crème fraîche in a bowl. Season. Cover and set aside.

2 Brush the capsicum and zucchini with 1 tablespoon oil. Cook the capsicum, turning regularly, for 5 minutes, or until tender and slightly charred. Remove; cover with foil. Repeat with the zucchini, cooking for 5 minutes.

3 Heat the remaining oil on the flatplate, then cook the onion, turning occasionally, for 5–10 minutes, or until softened. When nearly soft, push to the side of the hotplate, then add the steaks and cook on each side for 3–4 minutes (medium-rare), or until cooked to your liking. Remove the steaks, cover with foil and allow to rest. Spread the onion over hotplate once again, reduce the heat, sprinkle with sugar and cook for 1–2 minutes, or until the sugar has dissolved and the onion appears glossy. Add the vinegar, stirring continuously for 1–2 minutes, or until it is absorbed. Remove at once.

4 Peel capsicum, then divide among serving plates with the zucchini. Place the steaks on top, season and top with the balsamic onions. Serve with mustard crème fraîche and salad.

FILLET STEAK WITH MIXED MUSHROOMS AND SHERRY

SERVES 4

250 g (9 oz) broccoli, cut into large florets

250 g (9 oz) green beans, topped and tailed

1 tablespoon oil

60 g (2¼ oz) butter

4 rib eye steaks (scotch fillet) (about 160 g/5¾ oz each), 2.5 cm (1 inch) thick

3 garlic cloves, finely chopped

250 g (9 oz) mixed mushrooms (portabello, Swiss brown, shiitake or button)

2 teaspoons chopped fresh thyme

125 ml (4 fl oz/½ cup) dry sherry

1 **Bring a saucepan** of lightly salted water to the boil. Add the broccoli and beans and cook for 3–4 minutes, or until tender but still crisp. Drain.

2 **Melt the oil** and 20 g (¾ oz) of the butter on a barbecue flatplate. Cook the steaks for 3–4 minutes on each side for medium–rare, or until cooked to your liking. Remove from the barbecue, cover with foil and rest.

3 **Melt 20 g (¾ oz) of the butter** in a pan over medium heat. Add the garlic and mushrooms and season to taste. Cook for 3–4 minutes, or until the mushrooms have softened. Stir in the thyme. Remove from the pan.

4 **Add the sherry** and any juices from the rested meat to the pan and stir to scrape up any sediment from the base. Bring to the boil, then reduce the heat and simmer for 2–3 minutes, or until reduced to 80 ml (2½ fl oz/⅓ cup) and thickened slightly. Whisk in the remaining butter in small amounts, until glossy.

5 **To serve, put the steaks** on four serving plates, top with the mushrooms and spoon the sauce over the top. Serve with the broccoli and green beans.

STEAK WITH GREEN PEPPERCORN SAUCE

SERVES 4

4 x 200 g (7 oz) fillet steaks

30 g (1 oz) butter

2 teaspoons oil

250 ml (9 fl oz/1 cup) beef stock

185 ml (6 fl oz/¾ cup) thick (double/heavy) cream

2 teaspoons cornflour (cornstarch)

2 tablespoons green peppercorns in brine, rinsed and drained

2 tablespoons brandy

potato chips, to serve

rosemary, to garnish

1 **First of all,** bash the steaks with a meat mallet to 1.5 cm (⅝ inch) thick. Next, nick the edges of the steaks to prevent them from curling when they are cooking.

2 **Heat the butter and oil** on a barbecue flatplate over high heat. Cook the steaks for 2–4 minutes on each side, depending on how you like your steak. Transfer to a serving plate and cover with foil.

3 **Heat the stock** and stir over low heat until boiling. Combine the cream and cornflour, then pour the mixture into the pan and stir constantly until the sauce becomes smooth and thick — a few minutes will do the trick. Add the peppercorns and brandy and boil for 1 more minute before taking the pan off the heat. Spoon the sauce over the steaks. Serve with potato chips and garnish with rosemary.

BARBECUED CHERMOULA PRAWNS

SERVES 4

1 kg (2 lb 4 oz) raw medium prawns

3 teaspoons hot paprika

2 teaspoons ground cumin

30 g (1 oz) flat-leaf (Italian) parsley

15 g (½ oz) coriander (cilantro) leaves

100 ml (3½ oz) lemon juice

145 ml (4¾ oz) olive oil

280 g (10 oz/1½ cups) couscous

¼ teaspoon salt

1 tablespoon grated lemon zest

lemon wedges, to serve

1 Peel the prawns, leaving the tails intact. Gently pull out the dark vein from the backs, starting at the head end. Place the prawns in a large bowl. Dry-fry the paprika and cumin in a frying pan for about 1 minute, or until fragrant. Remove from the heat.

2 Blend or process the spices, parsley, coriander, lemon juice and 125 ml (4 fl oz/½ cup) of the oil until finely chopped. Add a little salt and pepper. Pour over the prawns and mix well, then cover with plastic wrap and refrigerate for 10 minutes. Heat a barbecue flatplate to hot.

3 Meanwhile, to cook the couscous, bring 250 ml (9 fl oz/1 cup) water to the boil in a saucepan, then stir in the couscous, lemon rind, salt and the remaining oil. Remove from the heat, cover and leave for 5 minutes. Fluff the couscous with a fork, adding a little extra olive oil if needed.

4 Cook the prawns on the barbecue for about 3–4 minutes, or until cooked through, turning and brushing with extra marinade while cooking (take care not to overcook). Serve the prawns on a bed of couscous, with a wedge of lemon.

BARBECUED SWEET CHILLI SEAFOOD ON BANANA MATS

SERVES 4

500 g (1 lb 2 oz) green prawns (shrimp), peeled and deveined, tails left intact

300 g (10½ oz) scallop meat

500 g (1 lb 2 oz) baby squid, cleaned and hoods cut in quarters

500 g (1 lb 2 oz) baby octopus, cleaned

250 ml (9 fl oz/1 cup) sweet chilli sauce

1 tablespoon fish sauce

2 tablespoons lime juice

3 tablespoons peanut oil

banana leaves, cut into squares, to serve

lime wedges, to serve

1 Place the prawns, scallops, squid and the octopus in a shallow, non-metallic bowl.

2 In a separate bowl, combine the sweet chilli sauce, fish sauce, lime juice and 1 tablespoon of the peanut oil. Pour the mixture over the seafood and mix gently to coat. Marinate for 1 hour. Drain seafood well and reserve the marinade.

3 Heat the remaining oil on a barbecue flatplate. Cook the seafood in batches (depending on the size of your barbecue) over a high heat for 3–5 minutes, or until tender. Drizzle each batch with a little of the leftover marinade during cooking.

4 Pile seafood high onto the squares of banana leaf and serve with wedges of lime, if desired.

MARINATED AND SEARED TUNA

SERVES 4

80 ml (2½ fl oz/⅓ cup) soy sauce

60 ml (2 fl oz/¼ cup) mirin

1 tablespoon sake

1 teaspoon caster (superfine) sugar

1 teaspoon finely grated fresh ginger

2 teaspoons lemon juice

4 x 175 g (6 oz) tuna steaks

1 tablespoon oil

coriander leaves, for garnish

1 Combine the soy sauce, mirin, sake, sugar, ginger and lemon juice in a jug. Place tuna steaks in a shallow dish and spoon the marinade over the top. Turn fish in the marinade, ensuring it is well coated. Cover and leave to marinate for 30 minutes in the fridge.

2 Preheat a barbecue flatplate until hot. Lift the tuna out of the marinade and pour the marinade into a small saucepan. Bring the marinade to the boil and reduce for 1 minute.

3 Cook tuna steaks for 2–3 minutes on each side so that the tuna is cooked on the outside but still pink in the middle. Serve with some of the marinade spooned over the top and garnish with coriander. Serve with rice and steamed vegetables.

BARBECUED SALMON CUTLETS WITH SWEET CUCUMBER

SERVES 4

2 small Lebanese (short) cucumbers, peeled, deseeded and finely diced

1 red onion, finely chopped

1 red chilli, finely chopped

2 tablespoons pickled ginger, shredded

2 tablespoons rice vinegar

½ teaspoon sesame oil

4 salmon cutlets

1 sheet toasted nori (dried seaweed), cut into thin strips

1 Combine the cucumber, onion, chilli, ginger, rice vinegar and sesame oil in a bowl, cover and stand at room temperature while you cook the salmon cutlets.

2 Preheat a barbecue flatplate and lightly brush it with oil. Cook the salmon on the barbecue for about 2 minutes on each side, or until cooked as desired. Be careful you do not overcook the fish or it will be dry — it should be still just pink in the centre. Serve the salmon topped with the cucumber dressing, then sprinkle with strips of toasted nori. Serve with steamed rice.

RIB EYE OF BEEF WITH SPICE RUB AND PARSNIP MASH

SERVES 4

4 x 280 g (10 oz) rib eye of beef, bone
  on (beef cutlets from a rack)

450 g (1 lb) parsnips, peeled and
  chopped

50 g (1¾ oz) butter

3 tablespoons thick (double/heavy)
  cream

1 tablespoon olive oil

SPICE RUB

1 tablespoon olive oil

1 tablespoon ground coriander

2 teaspoons ground cumin

2 teaspoons smoked paprika

2 teaspoons soft brown sugar

1 teaspoon garlic powder

1 teaspoon salt

½ teaspoon ground black pepper

MERLOT REDUCTION

250 ml (9 fl oz/1 cup) beef stock

250 ml (9 fl oz/1 cup) merlot or other
  red wine

1 teaspoon caster (superfine) sugar

1 **Combine all the spice rub** ingredients and rub mixture well into both sides of beef. Cover; set aside for 30 minutes.

2 **In a small saucepan,** add the stock, merlot and sugar and bring to the boil over a high heat. Reduce the heat to medium and reduce the sauce by a third. Season to taste.

3 **Put the parsnips in a pan,** cover with water and bring to the boil. Cook for 15 minutes, or until soft. Drain and purée in a food processor with the butter, cream, and salt and pepper, until smooth and creamy.

4 **On a barbecue flatplate,** heat the olive oil over medium–high heat and sear the beef for 4 minutes on each side for medium–rare, or until cooked to your liking. Remove from pan and rest for 5 minutes in a warm place.

5 **Spoon a dollop** of parsnip purée onto a warmed plate, top with a spiced rib eye and ladle sauce over the beef and around the plate.

ROSEMARY-SMOKED LAMB RACK WITH BROAD BEANS

SERVES 4

2 cups hickory woodchips
2 x 6-cutlet racks of lamb
4 very long rosemary sprigs
1 teaspoon smoky paprika
1 teaspoon salt
½ teaspoon freshly ground black pepper
1 tablespoon oil
1 red capsicum (pepper), quartered
500 g (1 lb 2 oz) frozen broad beans
40 g (1½ oz) butter
1 tablespoon olive oil
1 garlic clove, finely chopped
pinch of sugar
2 tablespoons chopped mint leaves

1 Soak the woodchips in cold water for at least 1 hour, or overnight. Drain and place in two small, disposable foil trays. Put a tray on either side of the grill in a kettle or covered barbecue. Preheat the barbecue to medium indirect heat.

2 Trim the lamb cutlets of excess fat, then trim and clean the exposed bones. Cut a shallow criss-cross pattern in the fatty side of the lamb. Using a thick wooden skewer, pierce two holes through the centre of the meaty parts of each lamb rack and insert a long sprig of rosemary into each one, all the way through. Combine the paprika, salt, pepper and oil in a small bowl and brush the mixture all over the lamb.

3 While the barbecue grill is heating up, add the capsicum, skin-side-down, and grill until the skin blackens and blisters. Leave to cool in a plastic bag, then peel away the skin and cut the flesh into long thin strips.

4 When the grill is smoking, stand the lamb upright in a large roasting tin, with the bones interlocking. Put the tin in the centre of the grill plate, then lower the lid and roast for 20 minutes for medium rare, or until cooked to your liking. Remove from the heat, cover loosely with foil and allow to rest. (If using a gas barbecue, put the lamb directly over the heat.)

5 While the lamb is resting, put the broad beans in a large saucepan of lightly salted boiling water. Cook for 2 minutes, then drain, refresh in cold water and drain again. Remove and discard the tough outer skins.

6 Melt the butter and oil in a frying pan. Add the garlic and capsicum and cook over medium heat for 5 minutes, or until fragrant. Add the broad beans, sugar, salt and pepper. Toss gently until heated through, then stir in the mint. Serve hot with the lamb racks on top, allowing 3 cutlets per person.

ROAST BEEF WITH BARBECUE SAUCE

SERVES 6

2 tablespoons paprika

1 tablespoon onion powder

1 tablespoon garlic powder

2 teaspoons sugar

1 teaspoon chilli powder

60 ml (2 fl oz/¼ cup) oil

1.5 kg (3 lb 5 oz) piece beef fillet

BARBECUE SAUCE

2 tablespoons oil

1 small onion, finely chopped

4 garlic cloves, crushed

½ teaspoon chilli flakes

1 tablespoon paprika

½ teaspoon smoked paprika

375 ml (13 fl oz/1½ cups) tomato sauce

125 ml (4 fl oz/½ cup) beer

60 ml (2 fl oz/¼ cup) cider vinegar

80 ml (2½ fl oz/⅓ cup) soft brown sugar

2 tablespoons Dijon mustard

80 ml (2½ fl oz/⅓ cup) Worcestershire
   sauce

1 Mix the paprika, onion powder, garlic powder, sugar, chilli powder, 2 teaspoons ground black pepper, 2 teaspoons salt and the oil in a small bowl. Rub the mixture all over the beef fillet, then cover it with plastic wrap and refrigerate overnight.

2 To make the barbecue sauce, put the oil in a small saucepan over medium heat, add the onion, garlic and chilli flakes, and cook them for 5 minutes or until the onion is soft. Add the remaining ingredients and 60 ml (2 fl oz/¼ cup) water, and let the sauce simmer over low heat for 20 minutes, or until it is slightly thickened. Season well and let it cool.

3 Preheat a kettle or covered barbecue to medium indirect heat. Put the beef fillet in the middle of the barbecue and cook, covered, for 40 minutes for rare beef. If you would like medium beef, roast for another 10 minutes.

4 Brush the barbecue sauce all over the beef fillet and cook it, covered, for another 10 minutes. Remove the beef from the barbecue, cover it loosely with foil and let it rest for 10 minutes before carving. Serve with the remaining barbecue sauce.

ROAST RACK OF PORK WITH CHUNKY APPLE SAUCE

SERVES 6

6 granny smith apples

90 g (3¼ oz/⅓ cup) sugar

60 ml (2 fl oz/¼ cup) white vinegar

1 teaspoon salt

2 tablespoons finely shredded mint leaves

1 rack of pork with 6 ribs (about 1.6 kg/ 3 lb 8 oz)

1 tablespoon olive oil

ROASTED VEGETABLES

2 orange sweet potatoes

1 kg (2 lb 4 oz) piece pumpkin

12 small onions

6 carrots

80 ml (2½ fl oz/⅓ cup) olive oil

6 garlic cloves, unpeeled

2 tablespoons finely chopped flat-leaf (Italian) parsley

1 **Peel apples,** remove seeds, and roughly dice the fruit. Simmer over a low heat with the sugar, vinegar and 60 ml (2 fl oz/¼ cup) water in a saucepan for 15 minutes, or until cooked through. Remove from the heat and stir in the mint.

2 **Score the skin** on the rack of pork in a diamond pattern, rub the oil over the pork, then rub the salt into the skin.

3 **To make the roast vegetables,** peel the sweet potatoes, pumpkin, onions and carrots, and cut into large, even pieces. Toss the vegetables with 2 tablespoons of olive oil, and season well. Trim root end from the garlic cloves, drizzle ½ teaspoon of oil over them and wrap in a double layer of foil.

4 **Preheat a kettle** or covered barbecue to medium indirect heat. Put the pork rack in the middle of the barbecue, cover it and roast for about 1 hour 20 minutes, or until the juices run clear when a skewer is inserted into the thickest part of the flesh. When the pork has been cooking for about 20 minutes, arrange the vegetables around the roast and cook, covered, for 1 hour or until they are golden. Add garlic; cook for 30 minutes or until softened.

5 **Squeeze the garlic cloves** from their skin, and mash with the remaining olive oil. Stir in the parsley and season. Drizzle the dressing over the roast vegetables just before serving.

6 **When the pork is cooked,** remove from the barbecue, and leave to rest, covered, for 10 minutes. Slice between the bones and serve with vegetables and chunky apple sauce.

ROAST LAMB

SERVES 6

2.5 kg (5 lb 8 oz) leg of lamb

6 garlic cloves, peeled

2 tablespoons rosemary leaves

1 tablespoon olive oil

1 Make 12 small incisions in the fleshy parts of the lamb. Cut the garlic cloves in half lengthways, and push them into the incisions with the rosemary leaves. Rub lamb with the oil and season liberally with salt and pepper. Preheat a kettle or covered barbecue to medium indirect heat, place the lamb in the middle of the barbecue, replace the lid, and roast for 1 hour 30 minutes.

2 When lamb is ready, remove it from the barbecue and let it rest, covered, for 10 minutes before carving and serving it with any juices that have been released while resting.

HONEY-ROASTED PORK FILLET

SERVES 6–8

1 tablespoon finely grated fresh ginger
6 garlic cloves
80 ml (2½ fl oz/⅓ cup) soy sauce
2 tablespoons oil
2 kg (4 lb 8 oz) piece pork neck or blade roast
2 tablespoons honey

1 Mix the ginger, garlic, soy sauce and oil in a large, non-metallic bowl. Put the pork in the marinade and turn so that it is well coated. Cover the bowl and refrigerate it overnight.

2 Remove the pork from the marinade, pour marinade into a small saucepan and simmer over low heat for 5 minutes or until slightly reduced. Stir the honey into the warm marinade and remove from the heat.

3 Preheat a kettle or covered barbecue to low–medium indirect heat, then put the pork in the middle of the barbecue and roast, covered, for 45 minutes or until cooked through. In the last 10 minutes of cooking, baste the roast all over with the reduced marinade. Remove the roast from the barbecue and place on a tray, covered, to rest for 10 minutes.

4 Carve the roast and serve with any pan juices left in the tray. Warm parsley carrots make the perfect accompaniment.

SIDES

BARBECUED CORN IN THE HUSK

SERVES 8

8 fresh young corn cobs

125 ml (4 fl oz/½ cup) olive oil

6 garlic cloves, chopped

4 tablespoons chopped flat-leaf
   (Italian) parsley

butter, to serve

1 Peel back the corn husks, leaving them intact. Pull off the white silks, then wash the corn and pat dry with paper towels.

2 Combine the olive oil, garlic, parsley and some salt and black pepper and brush over each cob. Pull up husks and tie together at the top with string. Steam over boiling water for 5 minutes, then pat dry.

3 Cook on a hot, lightly oiled barbecue grill or flatplate for 20 minutes, turning regularly. Spray with water during the cooking to keep the corn moist. Serve hot with knobs of butter.

BARBECUED BABY POTATOES

SERVES 6

750 g (1 lb 10 oz) baby potatoes, unpeeled

2 tablespoons olive oil

2 tablespoons thyme leaves

2 teaspoons crushed sea salt

1 **Cut any large potatoes** in half so that they are all the same size for even cooking. Boil, steam or microwave the potatoes until just tender. Drain and lightly dry with paper towels.

2 **Put the potatoes** in a large bowl and add the oil and thyme. Toss gently and leave for 1 hour.

3 **Lightly oil a barbecue flatplate** and preheat it to high direct heat. Cook the potatoes for 15 minutes, turning frequently and brushing with the remaining oil and thyme mixture, until golden brown. Sprinkle with salt to serve.

Note: The potatoes can be left in the marinade for up to 2 hours before barbecuing, but should be served as soon as they are cooked.

CHARGRILLED VEGETABLES WITH MINT AND FETA PESTO

SERVES 4

1 fennel bulb

12 spring onions (scallions)

150 g (5½ oz) green beans, trimmed

4 small zucchini (courgettes), quartered lengthways

2 tablespoons olive oil

MINT AND FETA PESTO

80 g (2¾ oz/1 bunch) mint, leaves picked

100 g (3½ oz) feta cheese, crumbled

1 tablespoon lemon juice

125 ml (4 fl oz/½ cup) extra virgin olive oil

1 Trim the base of the fennel bulb, remove the outer layer and cut the bulb into quarters lengthways. Cut out and discard inner core, then slice fennel into long pieces. Trim the spring onions, leaving about 7 cm (2¾ inches) of the green stem on top, and remove the outer layer from around the white base. Lay all the vegetables in a shallow non-metallic dish, drizzle with the oil and toss to coat.

2 Preheat a barbecue grill to medium. Grill the vegetables, turning occasionally, until tender and charred — the beans and spring onions should take about 5–7 minutes, the fennel may take up to 10 minutes. You may need to cook the vegetables separately if your grill isn't large enough to cook them all at once. Transfer to a serving platter and allow to cool slightly.

3 Meanwhile, make the mint and feta pesto. Put the mint, feta and lemon juice in a food processor and blend until roughly chopped. With the motor running, add the oil in a thin stream and blend until incorporated. Season with freshly ground black pepper.

4 Serve the vegetables hot or at room temperature, with the mint and feta pesto on the side, or dolloped over the top.

GRILLED HALOUMI SALAD

SERVES 4

1½ tablespoons lemon juice

2 tablespoons finely chopped mint leaves

125 ml (4 fl oz/½ cup) olive oil

2 garlic cloves

8 slices ciabatta bread

300 g (10½ oz) haloumi cheese, cut into 5 mm (½ inch) slices

3 ripe tomatoes

150 g (5½ oz) rocket (arugula) leaves

2 tablespoons pine nuts, toasted

1 Whisk the lemon juice, mint, 60 ml (2 fl oz/¼ cup) of olive oil and 1 clove of crushed garlic together, and season with salt and pepper.

2 Brush both sides of each slice of bread with 1 tablespoon of olive oil and season well. Brush haloumi with 1 tablespoon of olive oil. Cut the tomatoes into 1 cm (½ inch) rounds, brush with 1 tablespoon olive oil and season well.

3 Preheat a barbecue grill or flatplate to medium direct heat and chargrill the bread for 1 minute on each side, or until golden and marked. Rub each piece on both sides with the remaining clove of garlic. Wrap the toast in foil and keep it warm on the side of the barbecue. Chargrill the haloumi and tomato for 3–5 minutes on each side, or until they are browned, then drizzle with 1 tablespoon of the mint and lemon dressing.

4 Put the rocket and pine nuts in a large bowl, add the remaining dressing and toss gently until the salad is coated with the dressing. Pile some onto a piece of the garlic toast, arrange some grilled haloumi and tomato across the top and serve it warm.

ZUCCHINI WITH MINT AND FETA

SERVES 4

6 zucchini (courgettes)

1 tablespoon olive oil

75 g (2½ oz/½ cup) crumbled feta cheese

1 teaspoon finely grated lemon zest

1 tablespoon lemon juice

½ teaspoon chopped garlic

1 tablespoon extra virgin olive oil

2 tablespoons finely shredded mint

2 tablespoons finely shredded parsley

1 **Slice each zucchini** lengthways into four thick batons. Heat the olive oil on a barbecue flatplate and sauté the zucchini over medium heat for 3–4 minutes, or until just tender and lightly golden.

2 **Arrange the zucchini** on a serving platter and sprinkle with the feta.

3 **Put the lemon zest,** lemon juice and garlic in a small bowl and mix well. Whisk in the extra virgin olive oil with a fork to make a dressing.

4 **Pour the dressing** over the zucchini. Scatter with the mint and parsley and season with sea salt and freshly ground black pepper. Serve warm.

CHARGRILLED ASPARAGUS

SERVES 4

500 g (1 lb 2 oz) asparagus

2 garlic cloves, crushed

2 tablespoons balsamic vinegar

2 tablespoons olive oil

50 g (1¾ oz) parmesan cheese shavings

1   Break off the woody ends from the asparagus by gently bending the stems until the tough end snaps away. Cook the asparagus on a hot, lightly oiled barbecue grill or flatplate for 3 minutes, or until bright green and just tender.

2   To make the dressing, whisk the garlic, vinegar and olive oil. Pour the dressing over the warm asparagus and top with the parmesan shavings and lots of black pepper.

CHARGRILLED POTATOES WITH PISTACHIO SALSA

SERVES 4

750 g (1 lb 10 oz) potatoes

3 tablespoons plain (all-purpose) flour

2 tablespoons olive oil

sour cream, to serve

PISTACHIO SALSA

150 g (5½ oz) pistachio nuts, toasted

2 ripe tomatoes, chopped

2 garlic cloves, finely chopped

1 small red chilli, finely chopped

2 tablespoons chopped flat-leaf (Italian) parsley

1 tablespoon chopped mint

1 teaspoon finely grated lemon zest

1 To make the pistachio salsa, roughly chop the nuts and combine with the tomato, garlic, chilli, herbs and lemon zest. Season with salt and pepper.

2 Peel potatoes and cut into large wedges. Place in a pan and cover with water, bring to the boil and cook for 5 minutes. Transfer to a colander and rinse under running water to stop the cooking. Pat wedges dry with paper towels.

3 Sprinkle the flour over the potatoes in a bowl and toss to lightly coat. Cook the potato wedges in a single layer on a hot, lightly oiled barbecue flatplate or grill for 5–10 minutes, or until golden brown and tender. Drizzle with olive oil and turn the potatoes regularly during cooking. Serve with the salsa and a bowl of sour cream.

EGGPLANT, TOMATO AND SUMAC SALAD

SERVES 6

2 eggplants (aubergines), cut into 1 cm (½ inch) thick rounds

100 ml (3½ fl oz) olive oil

5 large ripe tomatoes

1 small red onion, finely sliced

20 g (¾ oz/⅓ cup) roughly chopped mint leaves

10 g (¼ oz/⅓ cup) roughly chopped flat-leaf (Italian) parsley

2 teaspoons sumac (see Note)

2 tablespoons lemon juice

1 **Put eggplant slices in a colander,** and sprinkle them with salt. Leave for 30 minutes to allow some of the bitter juices to drain away, then rinse the slices and pat them dry with paper towels. Using 2 tablespoons of the olive oil, brush both sides of each slice, then chargrill for 5 minutes on each side or until they are cooked through. Let the slices cool slightly and then cut them in half.

2 **Cut the tomatoes** into wedges and arrange them in a serving bowl with the eggplant and onion. Scatter the mint, parsley and sumac over the top, then put the lemon juice and remaining olive oil in a small, screw-top jar, season, and shake it up. Drizzle the dressing over the salad and toss it gently.

Note: Sumac is a spice made from crushing the dried sumac berry. It is a deep purplish red and has a mild lemony flavour. It is used in many cuisines, from North Africa and the Middle East, to India and Asia.

GRILLED PANCETTA, HALOUMI AND TOMATO SALAD

SERVES 4

100 g (3½ oz) pancetta, thinly sliced

2 tablespoons olive oil

1 tablespoon lemon juice

1 garlic clove, crushed

½ teaspoon chopped thyme leaves

200 g (7 oz) haloumi cheese, cut into
1 cm (½ inch) thick slices

250 g (9 oz/1 punnet) cherry tomatoes

1 baby cos (romaine) lettuce, leaves torn

1 Heat a barbecue grill or flatplate to high. Spread the pancetta slices on the barbecue and cook for about 5 minutes, or until crisp but not too brown.

2 Put the oil, lemon juice, garlic and thyme in a small screw-top jar and shake well to combine. Season well with freshly ground black pepper and pour into a shallow dish. Add the haloumi and tomatoes and toss to coat.

3 Spread the haloumi and cherry tomatoes on the barbecue, reserving the dressing. Cook for about 8 minutes, or until the tomatoes split and are lightly browned, turning often. Remove the tomatoes and continue grilling the haloumi for another 3 minutes, or until browned on both sides.

4 Put the lettuce leaves in a serving bowl. Break the pancetta into smaller pieces and add to the lettuce along with the haloumi. Leave the tomatoes unpeeled, but discard any skins which have almost left the flesh. Add the tomatoes to the bowl with the reserved dressing and gently toss to coat. Season with salt and pepper if needed, then arrange the salad on four serving plates. Serve warm.

GRILLED VEGETABLE SALAD

SERVES 4

1 red onion

6 small eggplants (aubergines), each about 16 cm (6 inches) long (not pencil eggplant)

4 red capsicums (peppers)

4 orange capsicums (peppers)

1 tablespoon baby capers

80 ml (2½ fl oz/⅓ cup) olive oil

1 tablespoon chopped flat-leaf (Italian) parsley

2 garlic cloves, finely chopped

1 Without slicing through the base, cut the onion from top to base into six sections, leaving it attached at the base.

2 Put the onion on a barbecue flatplate, with the eggplants and capsicums. Cook the vegetables over medium heat for about 10 minutes, turning them occasionally, until the eggplants and capsicum skins are blackened and blistered. Cool the capsicums in a plastic bag for 10 minutes and set the onion and eggplant aside.

3 Dry-fry the capers with a pinch of salt until crisp. Cut the onion into its six sections and discard the charred outer skins.

4 Peel the skins from the eggplants and remove the stalk. Cut from top to bottom into slices. Peel the capsicums, cut them in half and remove the seeds and membrane. Cut into thick slices.

5 Arrange all the vegetables on a large serving platter. Drizzle the olive oil over them and season. Scatter the parsley, garlic and capers over the top. Serve cold.

CHARGRILLED EGGPLANT WITH FRESH LEMON PESTO

SERVES 4–6

2 large eggplants (aubergines), cut into 1.5 cm (⅝ inch) slices or 8 small eggplants (aubergines), halved lengthways

160 ml (5¼ fl oz/⅔ cup) extra virgin olive oil

60 g (2¼ oz) basil leaves

20 g (¾ oz) parsley

50 g (1¾ oz/⅓ cup) pine nuts, toasted

2 garlic cloves

60 g (2¼ oz) grated parmesan cheese

grated zest of 1 lemon

60 ml (2 fl oz/¼ cup) lemon juice

1   **Brush both sides of eggplant** slices with 2 tablespoons of olive oil. Heat a barbecue until hot, and cook the eggplant slices for 3 minutes, or until golden and cooked through on both sides. If using baby eggplant, grill only on the cut side, and finish off in a 200°C (400°F/Gas 6) oven for 6–8 minutes, or until soft. Cover the eggplant to keep warm.

2   **Place the basil,** parsley, pine nuts, garlic, parmesan, lemon zest and lemon juice in a food processor, and blend together. Slowly add the remaining olive oil and process until mixture forms a smooth paste. Season with salt and freshly ground black pepper.

3   **Stack the eggplant on a platter,** drizzling some pesto between each layer. Serve immediately.

TABBOULEH

SERVES 6

130 g (4¾ oz/¾ cup) burghul

3 ripe tomatoes

1 telegraph (long) cucumber

4 spring onions (scallions), sliced

120 g (4¼ oz) chopped flat-leaf (Italian) parsley

25 g (1 oz) chopped mint

DRESSING

80 ml (2½ fl oz/⅓ cup) lemon juice

1½ teaspoons salt

60 ml (2 fl oz/¼ cup) olive oil

1 tablespoon extra virgin olive oil

1 Place the burghul in a bowl, cover with 500 ml (17 fl oz/ 2 cups) water and leave for 1 hour 30 minutes.

2 Cut the tomatoes in half, squeeze to remove any excess seeds and cut into 1 cm (½ inch) cubes. Cut the cucumber in half lengthways, remove the seeds with a teaspoon and cut the flesh into 1 cm (½ inch) cubes.

3 To make the dressing, place the lemon juice and salt in a bowl and whisk until well combined. Season well with freshly ground black pepper and slowly whisk in the olive oil and extra virgin olive oil.

4 Drain the burghul and squeeze out any excess water. Spread the burghul out on a clean tea towel or paper towels and leave to dry for about 30 minutes. Put the burghul in a large salad bowl, add the tomato, cucumber, spring onion, parsley and mint, and toss well to combine.

5 Pour the dressing over the salad and toss until evenly coated.

GARDEN SALAD

SERVES 4–6

1 green oak-leaf lettuce

150 g (5½ oz) rocket (arugula)

1 small radicchio lettuce or other red lettuce

1 large green capsicum (pepper), cut into thin strips

grated zest of 1 lemon

DRESSING

2 tablespoons roughly chopped coriander (cilantro) leaves

60 ml (2 fl oz/¼ cup) lemon juice

2 teaspoons soft brown sugar

2 tablespoons olive oil

1 garlic clove, crushed (optional)

1   Tear the salad greens into bite-size pieces. Combine the salad greens, capsicum and lemon zest in a large serving bowl.

2   To make the dressing, whisk all the ingredients in a small bowl until well combined. Pour the dressing over the salad and toss to combine.

Notes: Make the dressing and salad just before serving. Choose a selection of your favourite salad greens for this recipe. Add a sprinkling of chopped seasonal herbs.

COLESLAW WITH LIME MAYONNAISE

SERVES 4–6

2 egg yolks

1 tablespoon soy sauce

1 bird's eye chilli, finely chopped

3 tablespoons lime juice

200 ml (7 fl oz) olive oil

225 g (8 oz/3 cups) shredded purple cabbage

225 g (8 oz/3 cups) shredded white cabbage

160 g (5¾ oz/1 cup) grated carrot

180 g (6½ oz/2 cups) bean sprouts

30 g (1 oz) coriander (cilantro) leaves, finely chopped

4 spring onions (scallions), finely sliced

1 **To make the mayonnaise,** place the egg yolks, soy sauce, chilli, a pinch of salt and the lime juice in the bowl of a food processor. With the motor running, very slowly add the olive oil to the egg yolk mixture, starting with a few drops at a time. When about half the oil has been added, pour remaining oil in a steady stream until incorporated. Add 1 tablespoon of warm water and stir well. Place the mayonnaise in a bowl. Cover and refrigerate until needed.

2 **Combine cabbages,** carrot, bean sprouts, coriander and spring onion in a large bowl. Toss well. Add the lime mayonnaise and stir gently to combine.

GUACAMOLE

SERVES 4–6

2 ripe avocados, mashed

2½ tablespoons lime juice

3 spring onions (scallions), finely sliced

2 tablespoons chopped coriander
   (cilantro) leaves

1 teaspoon finely chopped red chilli

1 Combine the avocado, lime juice, spring onion, coriander and chilli, and season the mixture to taste. Cover guacamole with plastic wrap, resting the plastic directly on the surface of the mixture, and refrigerate until use. Serve on crackers or with thinly sliced raw vegetables as a dip.

TOMATO SALSA

SERVES 4

4 ripe tomatoes, finely diced

40 g (1½ oz/¼ cup) finely chopped red onion

25 g (1 oz/½ cup) chopped coriander (cilantro) leaves

1 tablespoon lime juice

1 Combine the tomato, onion, coriander and lime juice, season to taste, then cover the salsa with plastic wrap and refrigerate. Remove salsa from the refrigerator 15 minutes before you are ready to use it so the ingredients have time to return to room temperature and their full flavour.

SMOKY TOMATO SAUCE

MAKES ABOUT 500 ML (2 CUPS)

2 onions, quartered

2 red capsicums (peppers), cut into large pieces

2 red chillies, cut in half

3 tablespoons oil

3 garlic cloves, chopped

500 g (1 lb 2 oz) tomatoes, chopped

2 tablespoons Worcestershire sauce

125 ml (4 fl oz/½ cup) barbecue sauce

2 tablespoons tamarind concentrate (from Asian supermarkets), or lemon juice

1 tablespoon white vinegar

1 tablespoon soft brown sugar

SMOKING MIX

2 tablespoons Chinese or Ceylon tea leaves

2 star anise, crushed

1 strip orange zest

½ teaspoon five-spice powder

6 juniper berries

1 **Combine all the ingredients** for the smoking mix in a bowl. Pour the mix into the centre of a sheet of foil and fold the edges to prevent spreading. (This will form an open container to allow the mix to smoke.) Place the foil container on the bottom of a dry wok or wide frying pan. Put an open rack or steamer in the wok or frying pan, making sure it is elevated over the mix.

2 **Place the onion,** capsicum and chilli on the rack and cover with a lid, or alternatively cover the entire wok or frying pan tightly with foil to prevent the smoke from escaping.

3 SSmoke over medium heat for about 10–15 minutes, or until the vegetables are tender. For a very smoky sauce cook the vegetables for longer; if you prefer it less so, reduce the time. Remove the smoking mix container.

4 **Dice onion,** capsicum and chilli quite finely. Heat the oil in the wok. Add the garlic and cooked vegetables and fry over medium heat for 3 minutes. Add the tomato and cook until pulpy. Add the sauces, tamarind, vinegar and sugar. Simmer, stirring occasionally, for about 20–25 minutes, or until the sauce is quite thick. Store in the refrigerator.

BARBECUE SAUCE

SERVES 4

2 teaspoons oil

1 small onion, finely chopped

1 tablespoon malt vinegar

1 tablespoon soft brown sugar

80 ml (2½ oz/⅓ cup) tomato sauce

1 tablespoon Worcestershire sauce

1 Heat the oil in a small pan and cook the onion over low heat for 3 minutes, or until soft, stirring occasionally.

2 Add the remaining ingredients and bring to the boil. Reduce heat and simmer for 3 minutes, stirring occasionally. Serve warm or at room temperature. This sauce can be kept, covered and refrigerated, for up to a week.

INDEX